TOTALLY ■

twisted

innovative wirework
& art-glass jewelry

INTERWEAVE.
interweavestore.com

kerry
bogert

Editor and technical editor, Jean Campbell
Photography, Brad Bartholomew
Step by step photography, Joe Coca
Photo styling, Ann Swanson
Design, Lee Calderon
Production, Katherine Jackson

Interweave Press LLC
201 East Fourth Street
Loveland, CO 80537-5655 USA
interweavestore.com

Printed in China by C&C Offset

Library of Congress Cataloging-in-Publication Data
Bogert, Kerry.
Totally Twisted : innovative wirework + art glass jewelry / Kerry Bogert.
p. cm.
Includes index.
ISBN 978-1-59668-168-2 (pbk.)
1. Jewelry making. 2. Wire craft. 3. Glass beads. I. Title.
TT212.B64 2010
739.27--dc22
2009023670

10 9 8 7 6 5 4 3 2 1

contents

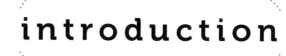

introduction

My path down the twisty road to wireworking started several years ago while surfing the Web. I was on a jewelry forum happily clicking links when one link led to another, and I found myself reading Connie Fox's *Brangle Bracelet* tutorial. I thought, *"Hey, I can do that."*

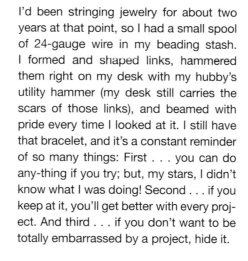

I'd been stringing jewelry for about two years at that point, so I had a small spool of 24-gauge wire in my beading stash. I formed and shaped links, hammered them right on my desk with my hubby's utility hammer (my desk still carries the scars of those links), and beamed with pride every time I looked at it. I still have that bracelet, and it's a constant reminder of so many things: First . . . you can do any-thing if you try; but, my stars, I didn't know what I was doing! Second . . . if you keep at it, you'll get better with every project. And third . . . if you don't want to be totally embarrassed by a project, hide it.

Within a few weeks of that first project, I realized I was addicted. I slowly started buying tools, new gauges of wire, and books, too. For some silly reason, I never thought to sign up for a class. I just kept blindly creating whenever I could. For me, it's the best way to learn and why I call myself *self-taught*.

Being self-taught, I've always struggled with the thought that I don't have any business telling others how to do things. Thankfully, I got over that enough to agree to teach. As I developed my class plans, I realized something . . . I don't do anything the "supposed to" way. Many magazines have a basics section that tell you how to wrap a loop. I don't do it like that. Many books tell you how to make an S-link and um . . . I don't do it like those either. But who's to say there aren't more ways of doing things than the supposed-to way?

I've now been working with wire for several years. I've taught loads of classes, written numerous projects, been published in all sorts of magazines, and been a contributor in several books. Why all the boasting? So you can realize that if stay-at-home-Mom me can do this . . . so can you! I have loved (and am still enjoying) my walk on the wireworking path, and this book is my next stop. I can't tell you how excited I am to share this with you.

My passion for glass and alternative techniques with wire are what you're going to find in the pages of this book. I hope you'll try the projects with as much enthusiasm as I had in creating them. But what I hope for more than that is that these pieces will spark your imagination and lead you down your own glass and wireworking path.

Go grab your pliers and get wiring.

kerry

the basics

Wire is an easy and fun medium that complements glass beads so well. I like it because it requires nothing more than a spool of wire, beads, and a few hand tools. The resulting jewelry is durable, wearable, and downright gorgeous.

materials

Most of the materials and tools you'll need for the projects in *Totally Twisted* can be found at your local bead shop or craft store. Start with the basics, then grow your stash as you go.

wire

This is the stringy stiff metal stuff you'll use in every project! It comes in a variety of **types**:

- *Anodized metal wire* is another name for the colored copper wire used in many of these projects. I prefer Parawire's colored copper wire for its durability and range of colors.
- *Sterling silver wire* contains 92.5% silver and 7.5% other metals, usually copper.
- *Gold-filled wire* is gold in color but is actually made from layers of 12k gold that are fused to a base metal, usually brass.
- *Brass wire* is stiffer than copper wire, but still very malleable and can be used for a unique aged look.
- *Copper wire* is the least expensive wire on the market, making it great for practicing techniques.

And it comes in many **gauges,** the way in which the thickness of wire is measured:

- *14-gauge* makes a great core for bangles and neck wires.
- *16-gauge* is my favorite size for clasps.
- *18- and 20-gauge* are great for making links.
- *20-gauge* is a standard size for ear wires.
- *24-gauge* is what I prefer to use for fine wire wrapping.

Note: The smaller the gauge number, the thicker the wire. For example, 12-gauge wire is thicker than 24-gauge wire.

And even **hardnesses:**

- *Dead-soft wire* is extremely malleable and can be bent easily into a myriad of shapes.
- *Half-hard wire* is somewhere between soft and hard; it's great for making head pins and ear wires.
- *Full-hard wire* is very stiff and can be difficult to work with; once formed, though, it can hold its shape under stress, making it work well for clasps.

You can work-harden soft wire, but it takes a torch to soften hard wire. I suggest buying dead soft wire for most projects.

beads

Beads are a great accent to wirework. Though there are hundreds of different types, I mainly used the following in *Totally Twisted*:

Lampworked beads. These glass beads are individually handmade with a torch and come in styles as varied as the artists creating them. These beads are perfect for wirework, as the holes can range from $\frac{1}{16}$" (1.5 mm) to 1" (2.5 cm).

Crystal beads. This type of bead is made from the most sparkling form of glass. They are cut and polished with many facets to reflect tons of light. Crystals come in a seemingly endless array of colors and have several different finishes. With so many to choose from, there is bound to be the perfect crystal to add glitz and glam to any project.

Pressed-glass beads. Usually from Germany and the Czech Republic, this type of bead comes in countless colors and shapes. They are made in molds for uniformity in size, shape, and design. The surface impressions left by some molds give the beads a look that begs to be touched.

Only Buy Annealed Beads!

Annealing is the process by which a hot glass bead is cooled slowly over several hours in a temperature-controlled kiln. Slowing the cooling process allows agitated molecules inside the glass to calm down and settle into strong rows. This makes the beads safe for use in jewelry. Make sure that the glass beads you're purchasing have been properly annealed in a kiln to insure strength and durability. Beads that are not annealed can easily crack, break, and even explode.

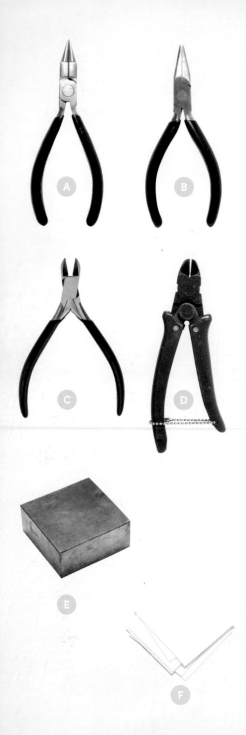

tools

Your first set of jewelry-making tools is an investment, and flipping through the pages of supply catalogs can be overwhelming. You need the right pliers or hammers to do the right job, but which one is the right one? There is nothing worse than spending hard-earned dollars on a tool that you just don't need (especially when you could have been buying more beads). The tools used to fill my wireworking toolbox are simple, inexpensive, and have stayed with me through years of beading. What follows here is a detailed list of exactly what you'll see on the desk in my studio, why I like it, and what it does. Keep in mind that some tools can be used for multiple things, and you can make a tool out of something you wouldn't expect.

A *Rosary pliers.* I prefer these to traditional round-nose pliers. The shorter jaw length gives you more torque when bending heavy-gauge wire, but can still make loops in any size you need. They also have cutters for quick snipping.

B *Chain-nose pliers.* My favorite grabbing pliers, I suggest you get TWO! I prefer these over flat-nose pliers because the narrow tips allow you to get into smaller spaces. These pliers are used for things like opening and closing jump rings, pivoting the heads of simple loops, and straightening kinks in wire.

C *Flush cutters.* Flat on the back, V-shaped on the top. A good sharp pair leads to less filing. My flush cutters tend to be my most often replaced tool. With the amount of wire cutting I do, they can become dull within a year. To keep the blades sharp longer, don't use these to cut anything other than wire. Don't ever cut memory wire with your flush cutters, it just isn't a pretty picture.

D *Big "Daddy" cutters.* Larger, heavier cutters for snipping thicker wire gauges.

E *Bench block.* For hammering and work-hardening projects. I like the basic 2" × 2" (5.1 × 5.1 cm) block. Stick with a simple square bench block. It's all you'll ever need when it comes to a surface for tooling wire.

F *Polishing cloths.* I like these little white squares for an extra shiny finish, but any type of polishing cloth will work. You can polish with these small squares until they are completely black and falling apart.

G Nylon mallet. This tool hammers and work-hardens without changing the shape of your wire. It can be very tempting to grab this hammer when you're hanging a new picture on the wall of your studio, but don't do it! The soft nylon head of this hammer can be damaged when not used correctly, and that damage can carry to the surface of your wire.

H Chasing hammer. These have a "ball-peen" (small, rounded) end and a "chasing" (large, flat) end. The ball-peen end is used to flatten wire and give it a tooled appearance. The chasing end flattens wire without leaving hammer marks.

I Tumbler and stainless steel shot. The number one way to work-harden and clean finished jewelry. Yes, you could use your kid's rock tumbler from the craft store. You could even tumble in the washing machine. Sooner or later, you'll want to upgrade. A one-barrel tumbler should work for beginners. To tumble a finished piece of jewelry, add 1 pound (.5 kg) of stainless steel shot, tap water, and dish soap to the barrel, then simply plug it in.

J Liver of sulfur. Available in chunks or liquid form, but I prefer the liquid. Don't like chemicals and the stink of liver of sulfur? Try using hard-boiled eggs! Read more about this technique on page 33.

K Coiling tool. This tool works great, especially for coils longer than 3" (7.6 cm). I really like the Coiling Gizmo. Every coiling tool works a little differently, so follow the directions included with your tool.

K Mandrels. I'm all about using what you have laying around before buying special tools. If you make lampworked beads, steel mandrels make great wireworking mandrels, too. A coiling tool is another fast and easy way to wrap wire. Knitting needles can be used as mandrels for coiling, as could the handle of a small paint brush.

L Files. I once read that you should invest in the best files you can afford. I say get the cheapest ones you can find and replace them when need be! I find my favorite files at a dollar store: emery boards—the type nail artists use to file acrylic nails.

Markers. Permanent markers can be used to write measurements on the surface of wire. This helps with consistent sizing for things like clasps and ear wires. The ink can be removed with a polishing cloth once your design is finished.

techniques

I find that all wire-jewelry projects are really variations of some very basic techniques. That means the basics are essential to learn and master. As the saying goes . . . practice, practice, practice!

I like the way sterling silver wire feels in my hands as I wrap loops, but when practicing, that can be pricey. Start out using craft or copper wire to make your test pieces. This way you can get comfortable working with different gauges of wire without worrying too much about cost. Each wireworking technique is the same no matter what size wire you use, but you may need to roll up your sleeves and muscle the wire a bit when working with those heavier gauges. I suggest trying these basics with 20-gauge wire to start and move up from there.

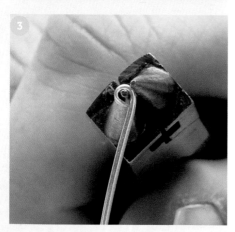

head pin

You already have a spool of wire on your desk . . . why wait for an order of head pins to arrive? Make your own; it's easy!

Supplies: wire, flush cutters, file or emery board, bench block, chasing hammer, round-nose pliers

1. Cut the wire into 2" to 3" lengths (5.1 to 7.6 cm) as needed for your project. File the wire ends smooth.

2. Set the wire on the bench block. Use the chasing end of your hammer to flatten one end about ¼" (6 mm).

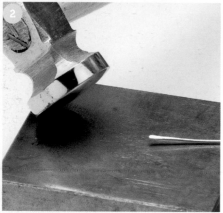

3. Use the tip of round-nose pliers to roll back the flattened portion so the wire end touches the stem.

There are a couple techniques required for any wireworking project:

Work-hardening, or hardening wire by working it, is done with a hammer or tumbler. Wire is malleable, meaning it can be bent and manipulated, so work-hardening ensures that the wire will hold its shape.

Flush cutting is a technique in which you trim the excess wire from your finished piece so the wire end is left flat, or flush. When you flush cut, make the cut with the flat side of the cutters toward the piece.

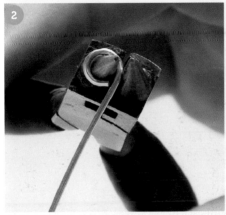

simple loop

Getting the measurement just right on these takes some practice, especially when you're creating bead links or eye pins. If I call for a simple loop in a project, don't worry—I'll give you the measurement and area of your pliers to wrap, so you can make the perfectly sized loop. When winging it on a project such as a basic linked bracelet, do a few test loops.

Supplies: wire, flush cutters, file or emery board, round-nose pliers, chain-nose pliers

1. Cut a 4" (10.2 cm) piece of wire; file one end.

2. Use round-nose pliers to bend the filed wire end so it forms a P shape.

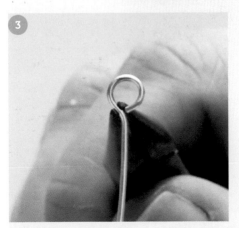

3. Use chain-nose pliers to grasp the P shape just inside the loop where the wire end meets the stem. Bend the loop so it looks like a lollipop.

4. To form a simple loop bead link, slide on a bead and repeat Steps 1 to 3 on the other wire end, working close to the opposite bead hole.

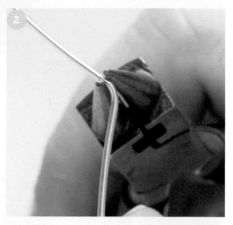

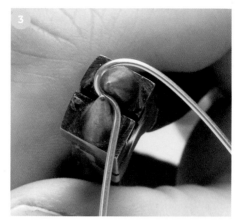

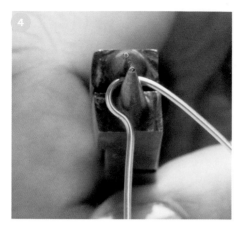

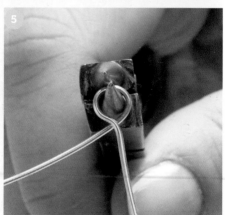

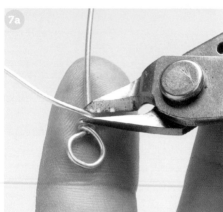

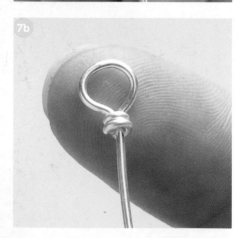

wrapped loop

Every tutorial I have ever seen for a wrapped loop uses multiple sets of pliers. Wrap with this, switch to that, back and forth. What a pain! My way of wrapping a loop uses just one set of pliers. With practice, you'll get it down.

Supplies: wire, round-nose pliers, flush cutters, file or emery board

1. Hold the wire vertically in front of you. Use your dominant hand to grasp the wire with round-nose pliers about 4" (10.2 cm) from the end. Use your nondominant hand to hold the wire stem just below the pliers.

2. Turn the pliers away from you about 45 degrees.

3 Keep the pliers in position as you use your nondominant hand to pull the bent wire up and over the pliers' top jaw, creating a shepherd's hook shape.

4 Remove the pliers and re-grasp the wire so the bottom jaw is inside the shepherd's hook.

5 Use your nondominant hand to swing the end of the shepherd's hook tight under the bottom jaw of the pliers. The wire should end up at a 90-degree angle behind the straight wire.

6 Wrap the wire end around the straight wire two times. Look, you made a wrapped loop!

7 Flush cut the excess wire close to the wrap. File any rough wire edges.

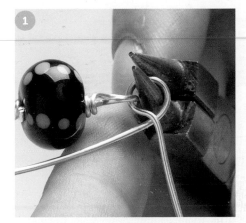

Wrapped-Loop Tips

Don't get frustrated if your first loop doesn't turn out perfect. These take practice. Here are a few tips to help:

- For your first few practice loops, give yourself some extra length to do the wrapping.
- If you want really consistently sized loops, use a permanent marker to mark your pliers and always form your loops at that mark.
- Keep in mind that when it's time to wrap the loop closed, you're coiling the wrapping wire around the wire stem, not twisting these wires together.
- Go slowly and keep practicing. Your tenth wrapped loop will be better than your first and your fiftieth will be better than your tenth. You have to keep at it!

wrapped-loop links

When you're ready to move on from making a wrapped loop and want to start linking them together to make chain, it just takes one extra step.

Supplies: wire, round-nose pliers, flush cutters, file or emery board

1 Repeat Steps 1 to 3 of the wrapped loop (page 14). When you adjust the pliers before wrapping the loop closed, slide the loop of a finished link onto the bend wire of the new loop. It will settle in the crook of the shepherd's hook. This locks the finished loop onto the new loop.

2 Finish with Steps 4 to 7 as you would a wrapped loop. Check it out—they're linked!

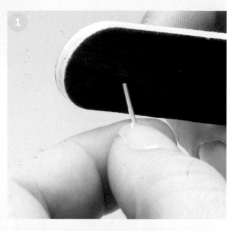

spirals

A wire spiral is a great, versatile technique that should be in every wireworker's repertoire. Finish them off with a simple loop to create cute dangles or add them to the end of head pins. The possibilities are endless.

Supplies: wire, flush cutters, file or emery board, round-nose pliers, chain-nose pliers

open spiral

This type of spiral has an open scrolling look.

1. Flush cut and file one end of a length of wire.

2. Use the tip of round-nose pliers to start a loop at the end of wire. *Note:* Make sure the wire is perpendicular to the pliers' jaws. If it extends out, you'll get a bump in your spiral.

3. Before this first loop reaches the straight portion of your wire, stop. If you go too far, you'll end up making an egg-shaped coil instead of a pretty round one. You need to think of this like a spiral, not a circle. Use your fingers to guide the straight length of wire around the outside of the starter loop.

4. Use the natural resistance of the wire to form the open spiral shape. Wire likes to be round, and it'll spiral nicely if you don't try to force it. Twist your pliers as needed to keep tips out of the way of your spiral.

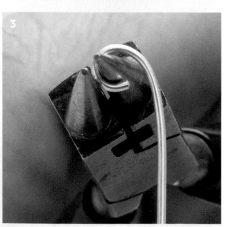

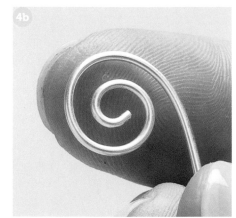

closed spiral

For this tighter closed spiral, you'll need to switch to chain-nose pliers after the initial loop.

1 Flush cut and file one end of a length of wire.

2 Use the tip of round-nose pliers to start a loop at the end of the wire.

3 Use the base of chain-nose pliers to grasp the first loop.

4 Use your other hand to guide the straight end into the spiral until you reach the size you need. Keep in mind that it never hurts to set the pliers down and do some of the spiraling with your hands.

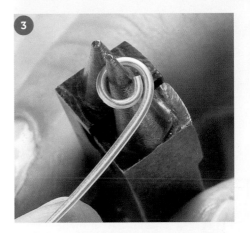

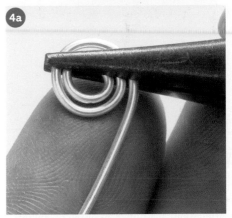

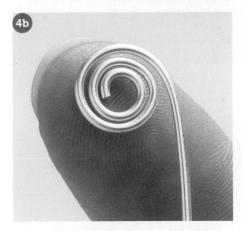

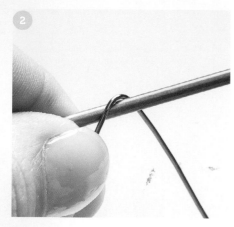

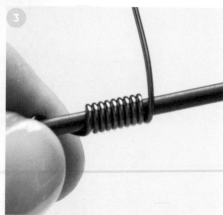

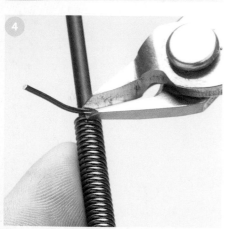

coiling

Just about every project in this book uses coils in some way or another. They're easy to do once you get the hang of it. I create coils by hand if they're under 2" (5.1 cm) long, otherwise I use a coiling tool (see page 11). Keep a container handy to collect short bits of leftover coil—they make great filler in all sorts of other projects. Keep in mind that the length and gauge of wire used to make a coil will greatly change the finished length of coil.

Supplies: 20-gauge wire, flush cutters, ³⁄₃₂" (2 mm) steel mandrel

1 To practice the technique, start with a 2' length (61 cm) of 20-gauge wire around a ³⁄₃₂" (2 mm) mandrel. *Note:* A 2' length of 20-gauge wire will produce about a 2" (5.1 cm) finished coil.

2 Hold the mandrel in your nondominant hand. Pinch the wire against the mandrel between your thumb and forefinger about 1" (2.5 cm) from the wire's end. Grasp the long side of the wire with your dominant hand about 8" (20.3 cm) from the mandrel.

3 Wrap the wire around the mandrel. Work slowly at first to keep the wraps tight. As you get into the rhythm of wrapping, you'll start to move faster. Loosen your grip on the wire in your dominant hand to keep your hand about 8" (20.3 cm) from the mandrel. If you get gaps in the coil, use chain-nose pliers to squeeze the gaps together as you go.

4 When just 1" (2.5 cm) of the coiling wire remains, flush cut the end close to the wraps. Flush cut any excess at the start of your coil, too. Slide the coil off the mandrel.

jump rings

Coils can easily become jump rings! Use the same materials and tools as the coiling technique with these differences:

Supplies: 20-gauge wire, $\frac{3}{32}$" (2 mm) mandrel, flush cutters

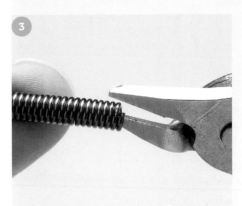

1 Make a coil with 20-gauge wire around a $\frac{3}{32}$" (2 mm) mandrel. Form as many wraps as you'd like jump rings plus several more.

2 Slip the finished coil off the mandrel.

3 Use flush cutters to cut jump rings from the coil. *Note:* The small jump rings shown here make fun embellishments on chain or in earrings, but you can make larger rings by changing the size of wire and mandrel. With larger rings, you'll notice that when you cut the coil you end up with a ring that has one flush-cut side and one side that's shaped like a V. To make both sides flush, turn your flush cutters and trim the V-shaped side flat.

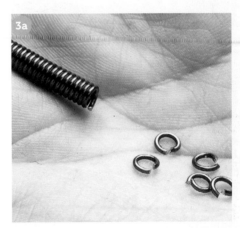

4 Use two pairs of chain-nose pliers to open and close the rings.

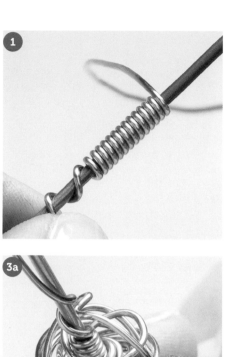

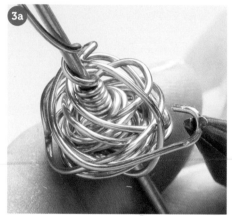

wire bead

Wire beads work great as fillers in designs that are short a bead or two or if you need to lengthen something. They also look great on their own. Wire beads are tremendously easy to make.

Supplies: 20-gauge wire, 1/16" (1.5 mm) steel mandrel, chain-nose pliers, flush cutters

1 Use 12" (30.5 cm) of wire to wrap the mandrel about fifteen times, creating a tight coil. This will become the hole in your wire bead.

2 Randomly wrap the wire back over the coiled area to build up layers of wrapped wire.

3 Use chain-nose pliers to add bends and kinks here and there as you wrap. When you reach the wire end, use chain-nose pliers to tuck the end into the wire bead.

4 Slide the bead off the mandrel. Use flush cutters to trim excess wire from the start of your inner coil after the wire bead is off the mandrel.

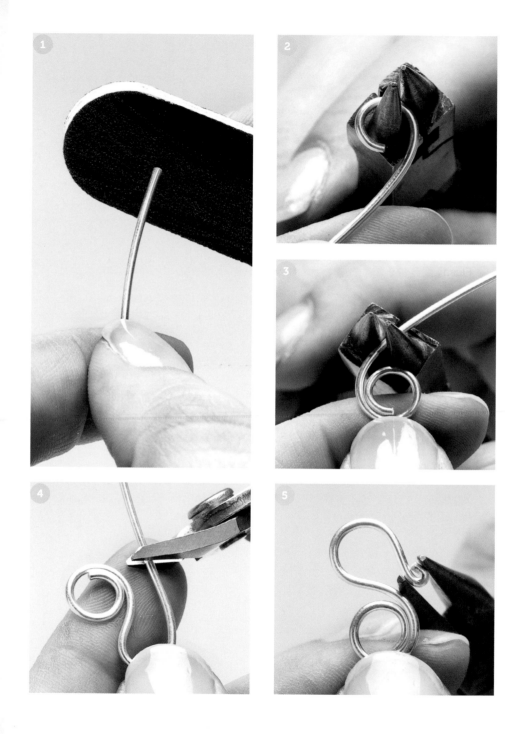

clasps

Most projects will need a clasp of some sort to keep them closed. You can make a bunch ahead of time and have them waiting for projects, or make them as needed. Here are three very basic clasps to get you started.

simple S-clasp

Simple, yes, but elegant, too. I love the graceful curves of this clasp. Experiment with the size of the hook to find a style all your own.

Supplies: 16-gauge wire, flush cutters, file or emery board, round-nose pliers, chain-nose pliers, nylon mallet/chasing hammer, bench block

1. Flush cut 5" (12.7 cm) of 16-gauge wire; file one end.

2. Use the base of round-nose pliers to start a closed spiral that has a large center loop. Switch to chain-nose pliers, if needed, to complete the second wrap of the spiral.

3. Reposition your pliers to form a hook at the other wire end.

4. Use the center of your spiral loop to judge where to trim the excess wire on the hooked end. Line up with the center of the loop, flush cut the wire, and file the end.

5. Use chain-nose pliers to bend the flush cut end back on itself.

6. Work-harden the arch of the hook and the spiraled area. Use the chasing hammer if you'd like a flattened arch, or use the nylon mallet to leave the wire shape as is.

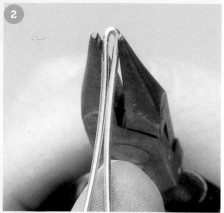

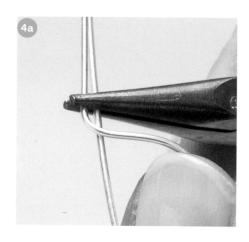

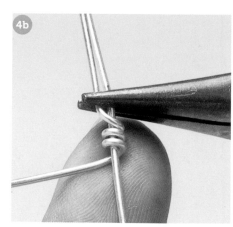

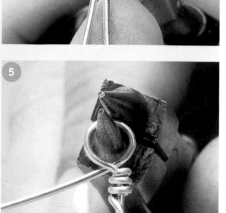

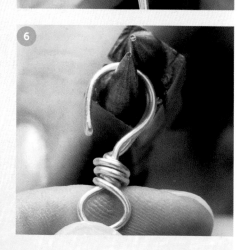

basic hook clasp

This is one of my favorite clasp designs. The extra bends and wraps give great depth that looks really fabulous when oxidized.

Supplies: 18-gauge wire, flush cutters, round-nose pliers, chain-nose pliers, file or emery board

1. Cut an 8" (20.3 cm) piece of 18-gauge wire.

2. Use chain-nose pliers to fold the wire about 3" (7.6 cm) from one end. Squeeze slightly to form a tight bend so the wires run side by side.

3. Use chain-nose pliers to grasp the parallel pieces of wire 1" (2.5 cm) from the fold.

4. Use your free hand to wrap the longer wire around the shorter wire as shown. Trim any excess tail wire.

5. Use round-nose pliers to form a wrapped loop at the end of the long wire. Overlap the first wrapping to give the clasp a chunky wrap look. Trim any excess wire.

6. Use round-nose pliers to grasp the folded wire at its mid-point. Form a U-shaped bend to create a hook.

7. Tumble the finished clasp to work-harden it.

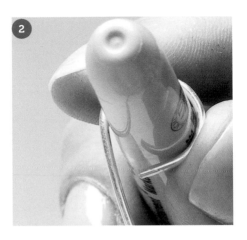

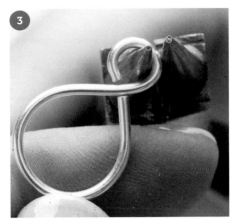

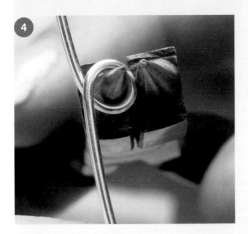

toggle clasp

This is a two-part clasp: a ring and a bar. Toggles are fabulously trendy, and this is an easy one to make. I have heard complaints that these easily come loose when being worn leading to lost bracelets around the world, but if you make sure the toggle bar is long enough, it won't slip out!

Supplies: 16-gauge wire, flush cutters, file or emery board, round-nose pliers, chain-nose pliers, chasing hammer/nylon mallet, bench block

1 Flush cut two 3" (7.6 cm) pieces of 16-gauge wire. File both ends.

2 Wrap one end of one of the wires around a child's marker or other ½" (1.3 cm) mandrel to form a large loop.

3 Use round-nose pliers to bend the opposite wire end, forming a figure eight. (I like one end to be larger then the other.) Set the ring aside.

4 To form the bar, use round-nose pliers to grasp the center of the second piece of wire. Pull the wire ends in opposite directions to create a loop in the center of the wire.

5 Use the tip of round-nose pliers to form a small loop at each wire end.

6 Work-harden both sides of the clasp by tumbling in a rotary tumbler or by using a bench block and mallet.

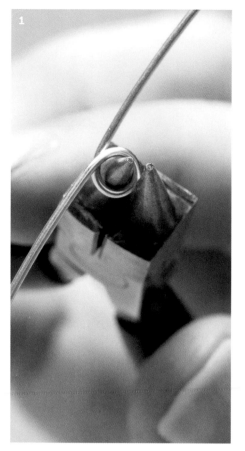

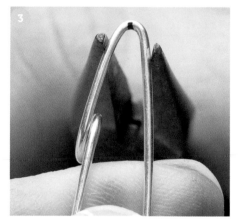

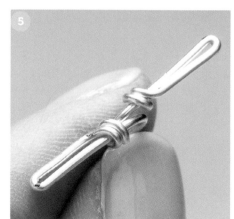

toggle clasp bar variation

Here's a fancier version of a toggle bar.

Supplies: 18-gauge wire, flush cutters, round-nose pliers, chain-nose pliers

1. Flush cut 6" (15.2 cm) of 18-gauge wire. Use round-nose pliers to form a loop in the wire's center.

2. Mark one of the straight pieces of wire about a ½" (1.3 cm) from the center loop. Use chain-nose pliers to fold the wire back on itself. The result should look like two pieces of wire running parallel to each other.

3. Use chain-nose pliers to pinch the wire fold, creating a tight hairpin bend.

4. Grasp the parallel wires and wrap the free wire end over the other as you would to close a wrapped loop. Trim any excess tail wire.

5. Repeat Steps 1 to 3 for the opposite side of the toggle.

6. Work-harden the toggle bar in a rotary tumbler for 30 minutes.

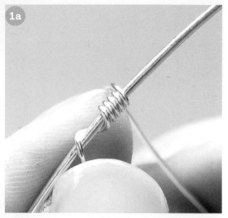

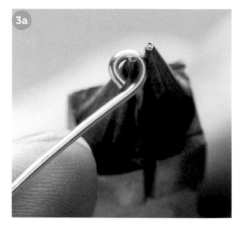

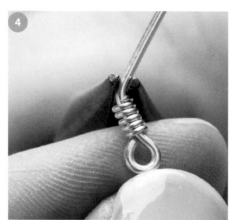

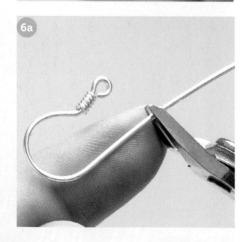

ear wires

Before going wild and crazy with unique, one-of-a-kind handmade ear wires, I think it's important to learn how to make basic ones. Yes, I know you can buy them super cheaply, and that's fine if you do. But I guarantee it'll feel good when you tell people that your earrings are entirely handmade, right down to the hooks.

fishhooks

This is an extremely classic and universally accepted style of ear hooks. They are easy to make and I suggest making several dozen at once so they're ready to use when you need.

Supplies: 24-gauge wire, 20-gauge wire, 18-gauge wire or ¹⁄₁₆" (1.5 mm) steel mandrel, flush cutters, file or emery board, round-nose pliers, chain-nose pliers, round pencil or other ¼" (6 mm) mandrel, chasing hammer, bench block, rotary tumbler

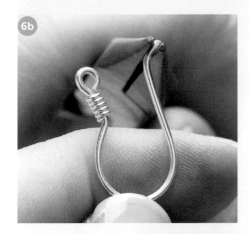

1 Coil 10" (25.4 cm) of 24-gauge wire around 18-gauge wire or ¹⁄₁₆" (1.5 mm) mandrel for a total of 10–12 wraps. Remove the coiled piece from the mandrel and trim it into two equally sized pieces. Set the coil beads aside.

2 Flush cut two 3" (7.6 cm) pieces of 20-gauge wire. File one end of each piece.

3 Use round-nose pliers to form a simple loop at the filed end of one of the wires. String one of the coil beads you made in Step 1, allowing it to sit next to the loop.

4 Use chain-nose pliers to grasp the wire firmly just above and tight to the coil bead. Form a 45-degree bend.

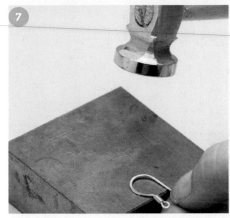

5 Wrap the straight wire end around the pencil or other ¼" (6 mm) mandrel.

6 Measure about 1" (2.5 cm) from the top of the arch and flush cut the excess wire; file the end. Use the tip of chain-nose pliers to form a slight upward bend ⅛" (3 mm) from the wire end.

7 Use the chasing end of the hammer and the bench block to slightly flatten the arch of the hook. Set aside.

8 Repeat Steps 3 to 7 to form a second ear wire.

9 Work-harden and polish the hooks by tumbling them in a rotary tumbler for about 30 minutes. When you're ready to use the hooks, simply open the loop to add a dangle (see Doodads, page 64).

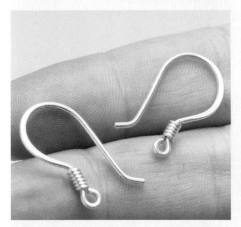

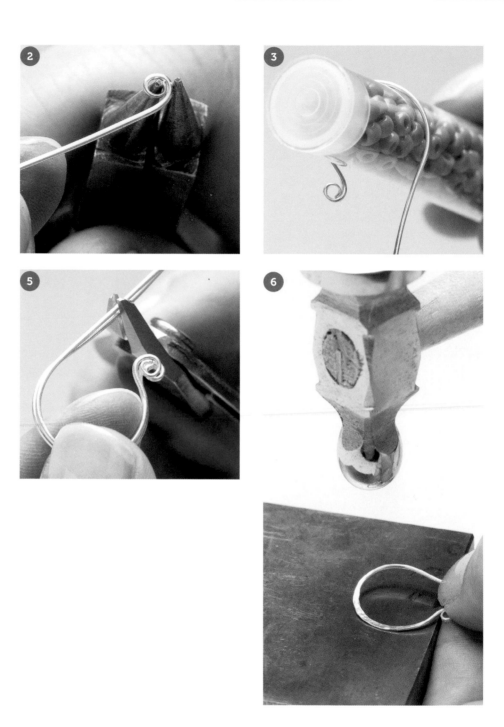

french ear wires

Want to add a little drama to your hooks? Go for the large loopiness of French-style ear hooks.

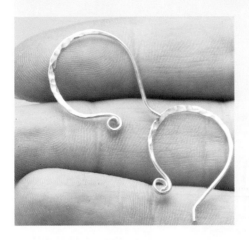

Supplies: 20-gauge wire, flush cutters, file or emery board, round-nose pliers, chain-nose pliers, 1" (2.5 cm) round mandrel, chasing hammer, bench block, rotary tumbler

1 Flush cut two 2" (5.1 cm) pieces of 20-gauge wire; file all the ends. Use the chasing hammer to flatten the first ¼" (6 mm) of one end of each piece.

2 Use round-nose pliers to form a loop with the flattened area of wire.

3 Wrap the straight piece of wire three-quarters of the way around the mandrel to form a loop. *Note:* Use your imagination and look for something around the house that will work as a mandrel. For example, use an extra-large permanent marker, a tube of seed beads, or a bottle of nail polish.

4 Repeat Steps 2 to 4 to form a second ear wire.

5 Measure about 1" (2.5 cm) from the top of the arch and flush cut the excess wire; file the end. Use the tip of chain-nose pliers to form a slight upward bend ⅛" (3 mm) from the wire end. You can trim both ear wires at the same time.

6 Work-harden the ear wires in a rotary tumbler or hammer them with a chasing hammer or a nylon mallet.

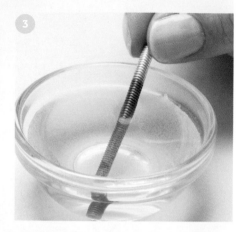

oxidizing

Have you ever opened up your jewelry box to add a new piece to your collection, only to notice that some of your pieces just aren't as bright as they used to be? Oxidizing is something that happens naturally to sterling silver wire over time. Slowly, but surely, the alloys within the sterling react to the oxygen in the air and blacken your bright, shiny wire or chain. To avoid the aging, store your finished jewelry in an airtight container when you're not wearing it. For some wireworked projects, though, oxidation can really enhance the finished look of your jewelry. Blackening your sterling wire on purpose, then polishing back the layers of tarnish will give your designs depth and highlight the work you've put into it. I love the look of oxidized wire for pieces with rustic and earthy bead color combinations.

liver of sulfur

Liver of sulfur is an oxidizing agent that's available in both liquid and solid forms. I prefer to use the liquid because it can quickly be added to a small container of warm water. You should always use liver of sulfur in a well-ventilated area. Once you're finished with the solution, add a few tablespoons of baking soda to neutralize the sulfur. After the fizzing stops, it's safe to pour the liquid down a drain with running water.

Supplies: small glass bowl, copper tongs, polishing cloth, rotary tumbler

1. For liquid liver of sulfur, fill a glass container with a few cups of warm water.

2. Add about 1 capful to the water.

3. Use copper tongs to dip your finished piece into the solution. Allow the piece to soak until the wire becomes blackened.

4. Remove the piece from the sulfur solution and rinse in cold water.

5. Use a polishing cloth to buff the highlights of the piece to give it extra depth and texture.

6. Use a rotary tumbler to further polish the piece.

the egg alternative

Liver of sulfur is very smelly and you may not want to keep it on hand if you only oxidize occasionally. Here's a great alternative that uses a few hard-boiled eggs. This process is slightly slower then a liver-of-sulfur patina, but just as effective.

Supplies: eggs, pan, water, stove, plastic bag or airtight container, fork, polishing cloth, rotary tumbler

1. Boil two to three eggs for about 15 minutes.

2. While still warm (but not hot, you don't want to burn yourself!), use a fork to break the hard-boiled eggs into large chunks, shells and all. Place the eggs into a zip-top plastic bag or other airtight container.

3. Add the finished wirework to the bag and tightly close. *Note:* You can just set your piece on the eggs; there's no need to mash the eggs all over the piece of jewelry.

4. Watch for the wire to blacken and remove the piece from the bag once it oxidizes.

5. Polish the raised surfaces with a polishing cloth; tumble as usual.

conquering
the color wheel

The way an artist sees color is similar to the way a musician hears pitch. When something is off, the maestro hears it. If a color isn't quite right, the artist can just tell. You don't have to be a maestro to conquer the color wheel, though. Here are several tried-and-true combinations that always seem to work and lend themselves to easy experimentation.

monochromatic

When something is called *monochromatic*, it's mostly one color with varying shades of that hue. You really can't go wrong with a mono-color look to a finished piece. There is one monochromatic rule in jewelry making, though. If you want people to actually wear your piece, don't pick an obnoxious tone as your base color. Choose something subtle and stay with the same color tone, adding different shades of that tone for interest. For example, if you're using lime green, go with lime, light lime, and dark lime. Personally, I love blue done in a monochromatic colorway. Oh, and don't get me started on purples!

accenting the opposition

You probably remember from one of your elementary school art classes that the three primary colors on the color wheel are red, blue, and yellow; their opposites are green, orange, and purple, respectively. Adding small accents of a color's opposite can be just the right touch to give a design pop. Stay away from using these colors in equal quantities, though. Remember that the opposite color is just used to add a touch of pizzazz, like a little coral orange to an all blue piece.

rule of thirds

This theory about color is my favorite and one I fall back on all the time. The

Rule of Thirds keeps your color pallet to colors no more then three spaces away from each other on the color wheel. That means if you're going for something in the green family, add blue and yellow or add blue and purple. If it's orange you're after, you could add a bit of red and dark purple, or yellow and light green.

temperature-telling colors

Red, orange, and yellow almost always call to mind a feeling of tropical-style heat and vibrant passion. Green, blue, and purple almost always give off waves of cool moisture and calm breezes. If you're looking to suggest a certain season or evoke an emotional reaction, keep colors in these hot and cold families. Then use the opportunity to mix different tones of that hot or cold color.

neutrals

I think this color pallet lends itself to being the easiest to work with in the bunch. Neutrals, in my mind, are best described as the colorless colors—they are more earthy and rustic in feel. All the shades of brown, any variation of ivory, and the lighter pale yellows are very neutral.

classic coordinators

There are countless color combinations that follow no rhyme or reason. They just look good together.

Here are a dozen of my favorites:

Purple and green
Hot pink, black, and white
Turquoise and orange
Shades of gray and yellow
Dark red and purple
Copper, green, and brown
Brown, blue, and green
Turquoise, brown, and ivory
Turquoise and cobalt blue
Gray, lavender, and teal
Shades of pink and brown
Black, brown, and ivory

ready-made palettes

I think a great way to work with color is to take inspiration from the experts, and a great way to start is to make yourself an inspiration board. Fill the board with magazine clippings that have colors you're drawn to, add fabric swatches that make you swoon, and collect images and color palettes from artists around the world.

My favorite way to stay inspired when it comes to color is contained in this mantra: *When in doubt, pull all the colors out.* I love working with bright colors, but as a rule, I never use all six colors (red, orange, yellow, green, blue, purple) together. I usually drop one or two and keep the rest, adding in a dash of black and white. For example, typical color palettes might be red, orange, green, blue, and purple; or yellow, orange, green, and blue. The most important thing about color is to have fun with it . . . to play!

bang gals!

Bangles are so much fun, especially when you wear several at once. In this loose-fitting design, big wraps of coiled wire twist along a core wire to add extra playfulness. Go wild with loads of color or tone things down with neutrals. No matter what you do, these are a BANG, gals!

materials

- 5' (1.5 m) of sterling silver 20-gauge dead-soft wire

- 7' (2.1 m) each of fuchsia and olivine 20-gauge colored copper wire

- 14" (35.6 cm) of sterling silver 18-gauge dead-soft wire

- 10" (25.4 cm) of sterling silver 14-gauge dead-soft wire

- 2 sterling silver 5mm smart beads

- 5–7 assorted 6×15mm to 10×18mm glass beads in variety of shapes

- 1 flower-shaped 18mm glass button with shank

Lampworked beads by Cassie Donlen.

finished size: 8¾" (22.2 cm)

Note: This longer length is due to the large swirl of wire. Though the bracelet measures 8¾" (22 cm), it wears as if it is a 7" (18 cm) bracelet.

TECHNIQUES

Simple loop
Coiling
Open spiral
Wire hook clasp

See pages 12–32 for helpful technique information.

tools

Flush cutters

File or emery board

Round-nose pliers

Chain-nose pliers

Chasing hammer

Steel bench block

Pint glass or bracelet mandrel

¹⁄₁₆" (2 mm) steel mandrel or coiling tool

Tube of seed beads

Rotary tumbler

Polishing cloth

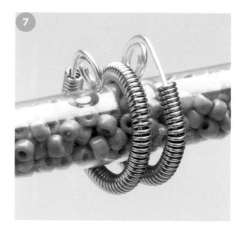

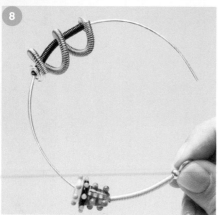

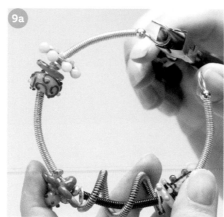

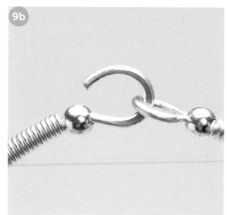

Will These Beads Break?

This is by far the most often-asked question when I sell jewelry made with glass beads. Glass beads that have been properly annealed in a kiln are very durable, though not indestructible. Normal wear and tear won't damage a glass bead. Treat them as you would any other piece of art jewelry (i.e., don't drop them on concrete or ceramic tile). Glass art jewelry can last for generations when worn with respect.

1 Flush cut a 10" (25.4 cm) piece of 14-gauge wire. File each end. This is the core wire.

2 Use round-nose pliers to make a simple loop at one end of the core wire. Use the chasing end of the hammer to flatten about half the loop against the steel bench block. Use the wire to string 1 smart bead; slide it to the loop's base.

3. Use the base of a pint glass (I found mine in a pub outside London) or other bracelet mandrel to form the core wire into a ring. The ends should overlap by 1" (2.5 cm). Set aside.

4. Use the 20-gauge sterling silver wire and the steel mandrel to form a 5" (12.7 cm) wire coil. Slide the coil off the mandrel and cut it into 3 even pieces, each about 1½" (3.8 cm) long; set aside.

5. Use the 20-gauge fuchsia wire and the steel mandrel to form one 1½" (3.8 cm) coil; set aside.

6. Use the 20-gauge olivine wire and the steel mandrel to create a 4" (10.2 cm) coil. Cut 7" (17.8 cm) of 18-gauge wire and form a two-wrap spiral that has a starting loop large enough to accommodate the core wire. String the olivine coil onto the 18-gauge wire. Form a spiral at the other end of the 18-gauge wire to secure the coil, but leave about ¼" (6 mm) wiggle room for the next step.

7. Use your fingers to wrap the 18-gauge wire around the tube of seed beads, forming a loose two-wrap coil. Use chain-nose pliers to bend the spirals so their holes are parallel. Trap the fuchsia coil inside this big twist of wire. Set aside.

8. Use the core wire to string 1 sterling silver coil and 2 or 3 beads. Pass the wire through one end spiral of the big twist made in Step 7, the fuchsia coil, and the other end's spiral. String the flower button, 1 sterling silver coil, 2 or 3 beads, 1 sterling silver coil, and 1 smart bead to add a total of about 8" (20.3 cm) of beads and coil on the core wire.

9. Use chain-nose and round-nose pliers to create a hook clasp at the bangle's open end (see *Basic hook clasp*, page 24). Hammer the arch of the hook to work-harden it, making it difficult for the smart bead to slide past. (Yes, it's a smart bead and should stay put where it is told, but sometimes they don't listen.)

10. Tumble the bracelet for 30 minutes then polish.

Double Spirals
For this version, make two wide coils instead of one, creating the second one with blue 20-gauge copper wire. Also substitute the flower button with 2 round beads and 1 disc. To make up for the additional wide coil, shorten each to 3" (7.6 cm) instead of 4" (10.2 cm), and make the core coils 1¼" (3.2 cm) instead of 1½" (3.8 cm).

alternate views

No Spiral
For this variation, leave out the wide coil. Oxidize and polish to highlight the coiling. After polishing, randomly wrap 20-gauge colored copper over the oxidized coils. *Note:* Don't polish the colored copper—the color might come right off.

butterfly

TECHNIQUES

Simple loop
Coiling
Open spiral
Wire hook clasp

See pages 12–32 for helpful technique information.

This is an ingenious design, if I do say so myself. It solves one of the age-old problems that many jewelry makers have: pre-sizing a bracelet. Inevitably, many designs, if they're not custom-made, end up too long or too short. With this clasp, you have sizing options. Pinching together the "wings" lengthens the bracelet, widening them shortens it. See? I told you it was ingenious.

materials

- 3' (.9 m) of sterling silver 18-gauge dead-soft wire

- 6' (1.8 m) of olivine 20-gauge colored copper wire

- 4 green/blue/pink 21mm lampworked flat rounded square beads

Lampworked beads by Sarah Moran.

tools

Flush cutters

Round-nose pliers

Chain-nose pliers

File or emery board

$\frac{1}{16}$" (2 mm) steel mandrel

Rotary tumbler

Polishing cloth

Liver of sulfur (optional)

finished size: clasp, 4" (10.2 cm); bracelet, 8" (20.3 cm)

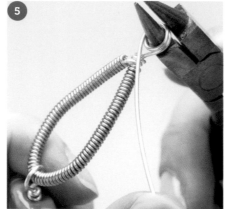

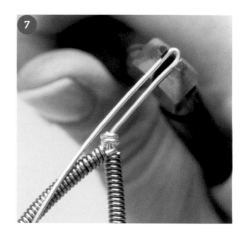

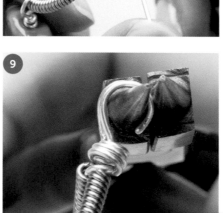

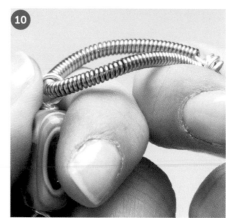

No Rotary Tumbler Nearby?

I recommend finishing projects with a rotary tumbler because it not only work-hardens the wire, helping it maintain its shape, but also cleans it, making a final polish much easier. If you don't have a tumbler, try using your washing machine. Place the finished jewelry in a sock or drawstring pouch and run it through a regular wash cycle with a load of denim or towels. When the load is done, so is your jewelry! No need to put it in the dryer.

1 Use the 18-gauge wire and lampworked beads to make a series of connected wrapped loop links (see *Wrapped-loop links*, page 15), creating a beaded chain 4" (10.2 cm) long. In order to attach the beaded chain to the clasp in the next steps, make the first and last loop in the chain larger than the others. Use the base of round-nose pliers to get the bigger loop.

2 Coil 3' (.9 m) of 20-gauge wire around the mandrel to create a coil about 3" (7.6 cm) long; set aside. Repeat to make a second coil.

3 Flush cut an 8" (20.3 cm) piece of 18-gauge wire. Slide one of the olivine coils onto the 18-gauge wire and use your fingers to form a U-shaped bend about one-third of the way from one end. Center the coil on this bend so there is about 2" (5.1 cm) of extra wire hanging out of the coil on one end and 3" (7.6 cm) on the other end.

4 Slide one end of the beaded chain onto the 18-gauge wire, letting it fall into the bend. Use the 2" (5.1 cm) length of exposed 18-gauge wire to wrap the giant loop of coiled wire closed, just as you would form the coil on a wrapped loop. Place the wrap so it connects the ends of the coiled wire.

5 Use round-nose pliers to form a large double loop with the longer wire end. To create a double loop, wrap the wire around the jaw of the pliers twice before closing the loop. Complete this loop with a chunky-style wrap, overlapping your first wrapping. Trim any excess wire with flush cutters and file any sharp ends.

6 Repeat Steps 3 and 4, adding a second coiled piece to the other end of the beaded chain.

7 Create the hook side of the clasp by forming a tight bend in the wire about 1" (2.1 cm) above the wrap made in Step 6. Use chain-nose pliers to pinch the bend so it looks as if two pieces of wire are running parallel.

8 Use chain-nose pliers to grasp the parallel wires just above the wrapped area. Use your nondominant hand to wrap the remaining length of wire over the first in a chunky wrap style. Trim the excess wire with flush cutters and file any sharp ends.

9 Use round-nose pliers to form a bend in the parallel wires, creating the hook.

10 Use your fingers to make a slight arch in the coiled loops so the clasp forms to the curve of your wrist.

11 Tumble the bracelet for 30 minutes, then polish.

alternate views

Create this version using emerald 12mm vintage crystal rounds, 16-gauge wire for the clasp's core wire, and seafoam-colored copper coils.

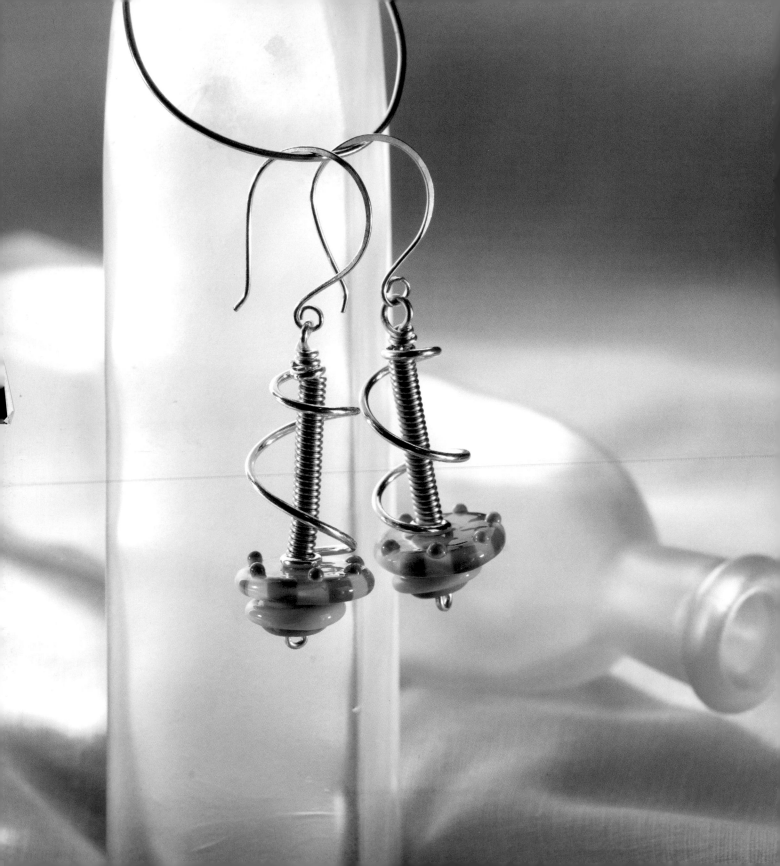

cagey

I love "caging" beads, a technique in which you use wire to wrap an entire bead from one end to the other, creating a cage around it. Something I like even better though, is to show off my wirework with an empty cage, as in this design. The final dangle reminds me of twirling kite tails and beachside wind socks.

TECHNIQUES

Simple loop
Open spiral
Coiling
Head pin
Wrapped loop

See pages 12–32 for helpful technique information.

tools

Flush cutters

File or emery board

Round-nose pliers

Chain-nose pliers

Rotary tumbler

$\frac{1}{16}$" (2 mm) steel mandrel

Polishing cloth

materials

- 8" (20.3 cm) of sterling silver 16-gauge dead-soft wire
- 8" (20.3 cm) of sterling silver 18-gauge dead-soft wire
- 6" (15.2 cm) of sterling silver 20-gauge dead-soft wire
- 2' (61 cm) of yellow 20-gauge colored copper wire

- 2 sterling silver ear wires
- 2 blue/orange 18mm lampworked disc beads
- 2 orange/green 12mm lampworked disc beads

Lampworked beads by Kerry Bogert.

finished size: 2¼" (5.7 cm)

This design is styled to match Twirl-A-Gig on page 132.

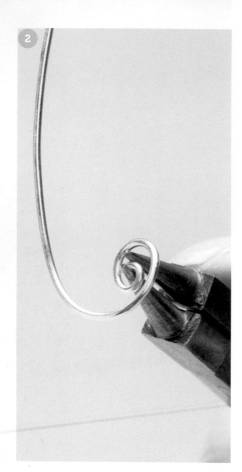

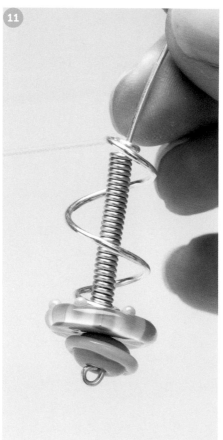

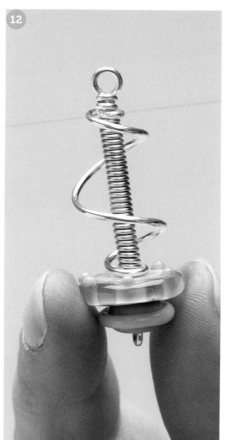

1. Flush cut two 4" (10.2 cm) pieces of 16-gauge wire. File the ends smooth.

2. Use round-nose pliers to form a simple loop at the end of one of the 16-gauge wire pieces. Let the wire's natural resistance help you bend it, forming an open spiral.

3. Continue spiraling until you reach the wire's center. Turn the wire over and form a simple loop at the other end. Spiral this side in toward the center. When the link is close to complete, put your pliers down and do a little hand forming. If necessary, adjust the bends so they are equal distances apart. Also make sure the simple loops are somewhat centered. Set aside.

4. Repeat Steps 2 and 3 to create a second cage.

5. Use the rotary tumbler to tumble the cages for 30 minutes. Set the cages aside.

6. Use the yellow 20-gauge wire and the steel mandrel to create a 2" (5.1 cm) coil. You could also use a coiling tool for this step.

7. Trim the wire ends and slide the coil off the mandrel.

8. Cut the coil into two 1" (2.5 cm) lengths. Set aside.

9. Cut 4" (10.2 cm) of sterling silver 18-gauge wire. Form a head pin.

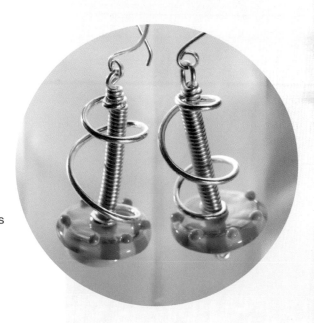

10. Place a cut coil inside one of the empty cages. Be sure to line up the cage's simple loops with the coil's hole. We'll call this "Coil 'n Cage."

11. Use the head pin to string the 12mm bead, the 18mm bead, and the "Coil 'n Cage."

12. Secure the beads and wire with a wrapped loop.

13. Use chain-nose pliers to open the loop on an ear wire. Slide the earring's wrapped loop onto the ear-wire loop; close the ear-wire loop.

14. Polish the earring.

15. Repeat Steps 9 to 14 to make the second earring.

catching
a wave

Seed beads are a wonderful pairing with lampworked glass beads. With countless colors available, it's easy to find a seed bead shade that will match perfectly with the lampworked glass. In this piece, we'll show off an amazing bead with some more subtle touches of wire.

materials

- 2' (61 cm) of sterling silver 16-gauge dead-soft wire

- 18" (45.7 cm) of sterling silver 18-gauge dead-soft wire

- 2' (61 cm) of 20-gauge dead-soft wire

- 5' (1.5 m) of Pacific blue 20-gauge colored copper wire

- 8' (2.4 m) of fine flexible beading wire
- 8 sterling silver crimp beads

- 10 g size 8° seed beads in cornflower, white-lined Capri blue, and chartreuse

- 1 green/blue/orange/white/black 45mm lampworked donut with 11mm hole

Lampworked bead by Libby Leuchtman.

finished size: necklace, 17" (43.2 cm); pendant, 3¼" (8.3 cm)

TECHNIQUES

Crimping
Coiling
Closed spiral
Wrapped loop
Hook clasp

See pages 12–32 for helpful technique information.

tools

Round-nose pliers

Chain-nose pliers

Flush cutters

File or emery board

¹⁄₁₆" (2 mm) steel mandrel

½" (13 mm) tapered mandrel, right-angle mandrel, wine bottle stopper, or the end of a fat paint brush handle

Crimping pliers

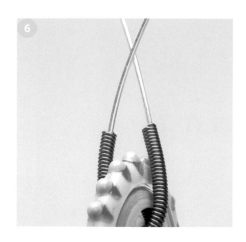

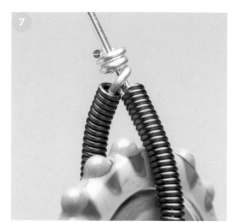

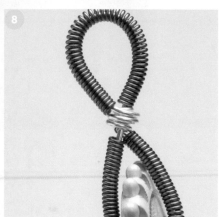

1. Cut 20" (50.8 cm) of beading wire. String 1 crimp bead; pass back through the crimp bead, forming a ¼" (6 mm) loop and leaving a 1" (2.5 cm) tail. Crimp the tube.

2. Use the beading wire to string 18" (45.7 cm)) of turquoise seed beads. String 1 crimp bead and pass back through the crimp bead, forming a ¼" (6 mm) loop. Crimp the tube. Set the strand aside.

3. Repeat Steps 1 and 2 to make 2 Capri blue strands and 1 chartreuse strand.

4. Use the blue 20-gauge wire and the ¹⁄₁₆" (2 mm) mandrel to make a 5" (12.7 cm) coil. Remove the coil from the mandrel and trim the ends. Cut the coil into two 2¼" (5.7 cm) pieces. Set aside.

5. Flush cut both ends of 8" (20.3 cm) of 16-gauge wire. Use your fingers to form a U-shaped bend in the wire about 3" (7.6 cm) from one end.

6. String 1 blue coil onto the wire and center it over the bend. String the focal bead over the coil, letting it settle into the arch of the wire bend.

7. Bring the shorter wire end to the center of the longer end. Use chain-nose pliers or your fingers to wrap the shorter end around the longer one so it's tight against the coil, just as you'd form the coil on a wrapped loop. Trim the excess wire and file the wire end.

8 String the second blue coil onto the bare 16-gauge wire. Make a bend in the wire as you did before, bringing the ends of the coil just strung together. Wrap the exposed core wire around the first center wrapping. Trim the excess wire and file the wire end. Set the bail aside.

9 Flush cut 8" (20.3 cm) of 16-gauge wire. Form ⅛" (3 mm) two-wrap closed spiral at one wire end of the wire.

10 Hold the spiral against the tapered mandrel about ½" (1.3 cm) from the end. Use the thumb on your dominant hand to hold the spiral in place as you use your nondominant hand to wrap the free wire end around the mandrel six times. The mandrel will taper your coil, helping form a cone shape.

11 Remove the cone from the mandrel and use round-nose pliers to finish tapering the narrow end of the cone. You want the hole in the cone's narrow end to be about ⅛" (1.5 mm). Trim the excess wire and file any sharp ends. Set aside.

12 Repeat Steps 9 to 11 to make a second cone.

13 Flush cut 4" (10.2 cm) of 18-gauge wire. Form a ¼" (6 mm) wrapped loop at one end, but before wrapping the loop, slip the crimped loop at one end of each seed-bead strand onto the wire. Wrap the loop.

14 Use the 18-gauge wire to string 1 cone from inside to outside so it covers the ends of the seed-bead strands. Form a ¼" (6 mm) wrapped loop to secure the cone in place.

15 Slide the top loop of the bail onto the seed-bead strands.

16 Repeat Steps 13 and 14 to finish the other end of the seed-bead strands.

17 If desired, make the necklace length adjustable by adding a 2" (5.1 cm) hand-made extender chain (see *Hook, Line, and Sinker*, page 116).

18 Use 8" (20.6 cm) of 18-gauge wire to make a hook clasp. Attach the clasp to one of the wrapped loops at the end of the necklace. The loop on the opposite side will act as the grab of your clasp. No need to tumble this piece, it's ready to wear!

chunky monkey

I love the weighted look of chunky wrapped loops. Using them as links looks extra nice with big beads since the additional wrapping helps balance the size of the beads with the thin wire. If you can make a wrapped loop, this'll be a breeze! Try this design oxidized with liver of sulfur for even more depth and texture.

materials

- 6' (1.8 m) of sterling silver 20-gauge dead-soft wire
- 2' (61 cm) of lavender 20-gauge colored copper wire
- 4" (10.2 cm) of sterling silver 16-gauge dead-soft wire
- 7 orange/blue/black/brown/red 15×12mm lampworked rondelles

Lampworked beads by Melanie Moertel.

finished size: 8¾" (22.2 cm)

TECHNIQUES

Wrapped-loop links
Wrapped loops, chunky style
Wire bead
Wire clasp

See pages 12–32 for helpful technique information.

tools

Flush cutters

Round-nose pliers

Chain-nose pliers

File or emery board

Rotary tumbler

Polishing cloth

Liver of sulfur (optional)

Balancing Wire and Beads

When deciding what wire gauge to use in a project, keep in mind that you want to balance your wire size with your bead size. Don't use thin wire with big beads or thick wire with bitty beads.

1. Flush cut 8" (20.3 cm) of sterling silver 20-gauge wire.

2. Begin a wrapped loop 3½" (8.9 cm) from one end of the wire. Form the wrapped loop as usual, making two wraps, but don't trim the excess wire. Instead, wrap again over those first two wraps. Since you're using 20-gauge wire, you may even want to triple wrap to get an extra-chunky look. If you're using heavy-gauge wire for this project, two extra wraps should be enough.

3. Use the wire to string 1 bead and finish the opposite wire end the same way. Flush cut the excess wire and file any sharp ends.

4. Continue building the bracelet, linking wrapped loops and wrapping them extra chunky. In my design, I also added a wire bead (see *wire bead*, page 20) to add a pop of color.

5. Make and connect your favorite style of wire clasp to the ends of the bracelet.

6. Use the rotary tumbler to tumble the bracelet for about 30 minutes.

alternate view

For this 8" (20.3 cm) version, use 2 matte smoke, 2 smoke, and 2 amethyst 12mm Czech fire-polished rounds in place of the lampworked beads, sterling silver 18-gauge wire for the links, and sterling silver 20-gauge wire for the 2 wire beads. Oxidize it in liver of sulfur for an aged look.

cluster
pendant

A sweet, cluster-style pendant is a must-have for every jewelry collection. Make the loop large enough to slide onto a range of different chains or cords. The fun shape of the beads used in this pendant make each one look like a bell ready for ringing. These are so easy to make that if you blink, you might have already finished it!

materials

- 15" (38.1 cm) of sterling silver 18-gauge dead-soft wire
- 12" (30.5 cm) of sterling silver 20-gauge dead-soft wire
- 2 blue and 1 purple ¼" (6 mm) 20-gauge colored copper wire coils
- 1 red/orange/green/blue 20×18mm lampworked cone bead
- 1 gray/blue 20×14mm hollow lampworked rondelle
- 4 lampworked 12×7mm rondelles in light blue, dark blue/light blue, coral, and tan/light blue
- 1 dark blue 13mm lampworked disc
- 2 lampworked 15mm discs in blue and light blue
- 1 green 18mm lampworked disc
- 1 chain necklace or neck wire

Lampworked beads by Kerry Bogert.

finished size: 3" (7.6 cm)

Reduce, Reuse, Recycle!

Scraps add up quickly when you work with wire. There's no way to tell exactly how much wire you'll need for any given link because each person's wrapping style is a little different. Keep a box for scraps handy to collect the bits and bobs left over from your projects. Short lengths of coil can be reused for projects like this one. Many companies also offer refunds or store credit for raw materials like sterling silver scraps, and that, my friend, is beads in the bank!

1. Flush cut 6" (15.2 cm) of 18-gauge wire. Form a ¼" (6 mm) wide wrapped loop at one end. This large bottom loop will accommodate the dangles formed in later steps.

2. Use the wire to string the hollow lampworked bead, 1 blue coil, and the cone bead. Form another ¼" (6 mm) wide wrapped loop at this end. This loop will be the bail for your finished pendant so it can hang from a chain. Set aside.

3. Use the 18-gauge wire to form 4 head pins. Set aside.

4. Use 1 head pin to string the orange rondelle and both 15mm discs. Form a wrapped loop that attaches to the bottom loop created in Step 2.

5. Repeat Step 4, using head pins to make dangles and attaching them to the same bottom loop. Vary the sizes of the dangles by changing the number of beads or adding coils.

6. Tumble the pendant for 30 minutes.

7. Slide the bail loop onto a chain.

delightful

TECHNIQUES

Coiling
Spiral
Wrapped loop
Wrapped-loop links
Simple loop beaded link
Hook clasp

See pages 12–32 for helpful technique information.

tools

This design is a throwback to a time when people found a way to use every part of everything. A catch-all of sorts for saved leftover beads and too-short lengths of chain. Though vintage-inspired, I think you'll find this necklace has a modern feel and is just oh, so, delightful.

Flush cutters

Chain-nose pliers

File or emery board

10 mm mandrel or marker

Chasing hammer

Steel bench block

Round-nose pliers

Rotary tumbler

Polishing cloth

materials

- 46" (1.2 m) of sterling silver 18-gauge dead-soft wire
- 14" (35.6 cm) of 4mm to 7mm sterling silver chain
- 3 blue 9mm anodized aluminum jump rings
- 1 blue 6mm colored coil length
- 3 Pacific green 16mm colored coil lengths
- 1 dark blue polka-dotted 12×7mm lampworked rondelle

Lampworked beads by Kerry Bogert.

- 3 cornflower 12×10mm lampworked rondelles
- 1 light gray-green 13mm lampworked round
- 1 green polka-dotted 13×8mm squared lampworked rondelle
- 3 assorted green and blue 15×10mm lampworked rondelles
- 1 blue and green 30mm lampworked lentil bead
- 1 g lavender-lined clear size 8° seed beads

finished size: 18" (45.7 cm)

61

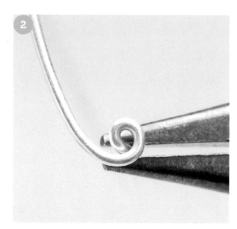

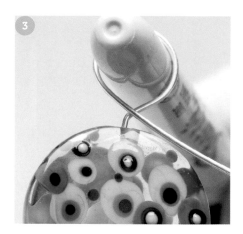

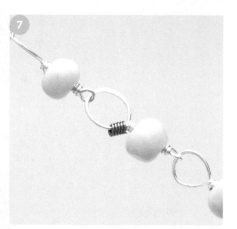

1 Flush cut 7" (17.8 cm) of 18-gauge wire. Use chain-nose pliers to form a 90-degree bend 2" (5.1 cm) from one wire end.

2 Hold the long portion of the wire firmly with chain-nose pliers just below the bend. Begin forming a spiral perpendicular to the long wire.

Once the spiral starts taking shape, move the chain-nose pliers to grasp the spiral so you can keep coaxing the wire into shape. Repeat until the short wire is completely spiraled. Flush cut the wire end so it flows with the spiral; file the sharp end.

3 Use the spiral head pin created in Step 2 to string the lentil bead. Use the mandrel to form a ½" (1.3 cm) wrapped loop, locking the bead in place to create the focal pendant.

4 Hammer the pendant's wrapped loop against the bench block to flatten or texture the wire. Be sure to hang the focal bead off the side of the bench block so it doesn't get hit by the hammer and break.

5 Flush cut 5" (12.7 cm) of 18-gauge wire. Form a ⅛" (3 mm) wrapped loop at one end. Before wrapping the loop, attach it to the pendant's loop.

6 String 1 cornflower rondelle onto the wire and use the mandrel to form a ½" (1.3 cm) wrapped loop. Hammer this loop as you did before.

7 Repeat Step 4 three more times, connecting each new link to the large loop of the one before, until you have a beaded chain 4 links long. Use the squared rondelle for the final link. Add some interest to the design by including the blue coil to the second link and 2 seed beads to the fourth link before wrapping the loops closed. Be sure to slide any added embellishments to the side before hammering the loops on the bench block.

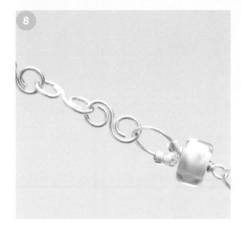

8 Open the end link of 5" (12.7 cm) of sterling silver chain and attach to the last loop of the beaded chain. (The chain shown is from *Lasso*, page 84.) The last loop of this chain will act as the ring side of your clasp.

9 Use 1 colored jump ring to attach the end link of a 4" (10.2 cm) sterling silver chain to the pendant's loop; repeat to add a second chain. To create the colored coil chain links, cut 2" (5.1 cm) of 20-gauge wire and form a 3mm simple loop on one end of the wire. String a 1" (2.5 cm) length of coil. Trim the wire end to ¼" (6 mm) and form a second simple loop; set aside. Repeat to create 2 more links. Connect links by opening the simple loop on one side of the link and attaching it to the next link. *Note:* The chains shown are from *Hook, Line, and Sinker* (page 116) and *Squiggle Wiggle* (page 68), but commercial chains are also fine to use. The main thing is to use 2 chain lengths side by side to help balance the weight of the beaded links on the opposite side of the necklace. Set the necklace aside.

10 Use 18-gauge wire and the remaining beads to make a chain with simple loop beaded links, 1 bead per link. Use 1 jump ring to attach the beaded chain to the end links of the chains placed in Step 9.

11 Use 18-gauge wire to form a hook clasp. Attach it to the end of the simple loop beaded chain.

12 Tumble the necklace for 45 minutes, then polish.

doodads

What better way to make earrings than with an easy dangle? This is a truly timeless design that's been around for centuries and will be around at least a few hundred more. The beads you choose and the length you make them are just two ways you can set your designs apart from the crowd. And don't forget to tell the crowd that you made them from scratch!

materials

- 12" (30.5 cm) of sterling silver 20-gauge dead-soft wire
- 2 sets of assorted 9×13mm to 11×14mm beads

Lampworked beads by Kerry Bogert.

finished size: 1¼" (3.2 cm)

TECHNIQUES

Simple loop
French hooks
Fish hooks

See pages 12–32 for helpful technique information.

tools

Flush cutters

File or emery board

Round-nose pliers

Chain-nose pliers

Chasing hammer or nylon mallet

Bench block

Rotary tumbler

Polishing cloth

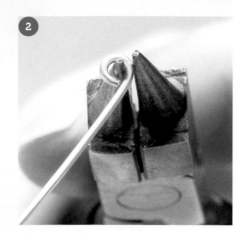

1 Use the 20-gauge wire to make 2 fishhook ear wires. Set them aside.

2 Flush cut 4" (7.6 cm) of wire. File the ends smooth. Form a simple loop at one end; set aside. Repeat to make a second eye pin.

3 String your desired beads on 1 eye pin, leaving at least ⅜" (9 mm) of exposed wire. Form a simple or wrapped loop to lock the beads in place; set the dangle aside. Repeat for the second eye pin.

4 Use chain-nose pliers to open the loop of an ear wire. *Note:* Be sure to open the loop side to side, not out; opening it incorrectly will misshape the wire, creating a very sloppy loop.

5 Slide 1 dangle onto the loop; close the loop.

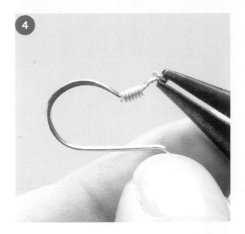

Closing Loops

To get a good close on a simple loop or jump ring, shimmy the wire end past where you want it to be. It will spring back into the right spot. Try it and you'll see what I mean.

6 Repeat Steps 4 and 5 to assemble the second earring.

7 Tumble the earrings for 30 minutes, then polish.

squiggle
wiggle

Lariat necklaces were quite popular with flappers in the 1920s. I've given this classic style a modern makeover using lampworked glass and wire, creating a long enough chain to wrap the neck twice and still leave room for the free ends to dangle like pendants.

materials

- 2' (61 cm) of sterling silver 16-gauge dead-soft wire

- 12' (3.7 cm) of sterling silver 20-gauge dead-soft wire

- 20' (6.1 m) of burgundy 20-gauge colored copper wire

- 2 burgundy/green/orange/blue 15×23mm lampworked glass drop beads

- 1 burgundy/green/orange/blue 29×15mm lampworked glass pointed oval bead

Lampworked beads by Sarah Moran.

finished size: 34½" (87.6 cm)

TECHNIQUES

Coiling
Simple loop
Wrapped loop

See pages 12–32 for helpful technique information.

tools

¹⁄₁₆" (2 mm) steel mandrel

Flush cutters

Round-nose pliers

Chain-nose pliers

File or emery board

Nail polish bottle

Rotary tumbler

Polishing cloth

3

5

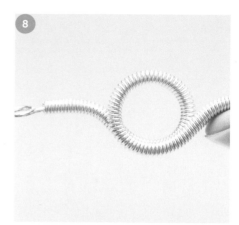

8

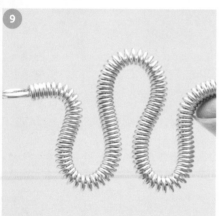

9

12

13

Consistent Loops

Want your loops to turn out all the same size? Mark the area you use to wrap the loop on your pliers with a permanent marker. If you always wrap at the same spot, they will all turn out the same size!

1. Use the burgundy wire and steel mandrel to form a 1" (2.5 cm) coil. Slide the coil off the mandrel, trim the ends, and set aside. Repeat to make a total of 20 coils.

2. Flush cut 2" (5.1 cm) of sterling silver 20-gauge wire. Form a simple loop at one end.

3. Slide 1 burgundy coil onto the silver wire. Trim the silver wire so ½" (1.3 cm) extends past the coil. Form another simple loop. Set the coiled link aside.

4. Repeat Steps 2 and 3 to form a total of 20 coiled links.

5. Use chain-nose pliers to open one of the coiled link loops and attach it to a loop of another link. Close the loop. Repeat to connect all 20 links. Set the chain aside.

6. Use 4' (1.2 cm) of silver 20-gauge wire and the mandrel to form a 4" (10.2 cm) coil. Slide the coil off the mandrel, trim the ends, and set aside. Repeat to make a second coil.

7. Flush cut 6" (15.2 cm) of 16-gauge wire and file each end. Form a simple loop at one end. Slide on the 4" (10.2 cm) coil and form another simple loop, leaving a little wiggle room between the loop and coil. Repeat to make a second coiled link.

8. Hold the coiled link perpendicular to the top of the nail polish bottle. Use the bottle top as a mandrel as you wrap the coiled link around the bottle top twice. Use your fingers to straighten the wire ends. Set this squiggle link aside.

9. Wrap the first third of the second coiled link halfway around the bottle top. Do the same thing in the opposite direction with the link's middle third, then again in the opposite direction for the last third of the link to form a cursive W shape. Use your fingers to pinch together the bends of the wire coil, compacting the shape.

10. Use chain-nose pliers to open one of the simple loops of the link just formed and attach it to one of the chain ends; close the loop. Do the same with the second squiggle link, adding it to the opposite chain end. Set aside.

11. Flush cut 5" (12.7 cm) of 16-gauge wire. Form a wrapped loop that attaches to the drop bead. Trim any excess tail wire and file the end if needed.

12. String the pointed oval bead onto the wire and form a wrapped loop to lock it in place. Attach this dangle to the simple loop at the end of one of the squiggle links.

13. Repeat Step 11. Form a wrapped loop that attaches to the second drop bead. Trim any excess tail and file if needed. Trim the remaining wire to ¾" (1.9 cm) and form a simple loop close to the previous loop's coils. Attach the dangle to the simple loop at the end of the other squiggle link.

14. Tumble the lariat for 30 minutes, then polish.

alternate views

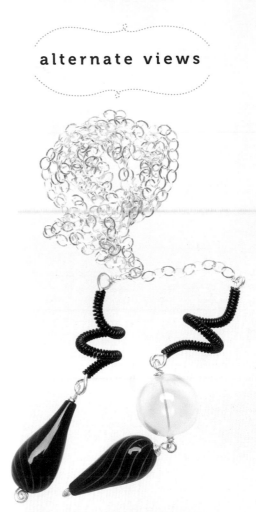

This lariat is even longer than the one shown on page 68. Measuring out at 47½" (1.2 m), this lariat can be wrapped several times around the neck. It's made up of premade chain, 1 clear 20mm round, and 2 red 14×30mm blown-glass drop beads.

fantasticness

This simple bracelet design lets you highlight a single art bead and show off a bit of handmade wire chain. Keep the fit tight, and the bead will stay right on top of your wrist where it can be properly admired. A double strand of this dainty style chain will help balance out the overall size of the finished piece.

materials

- 5' (1.5 m) of sterling silver 18-gauge dead-soft wire
- 1 blue/black 18mm lampworked pillow bead
- 1 wire toggle clasp

Lampworked beads by Anne Ricketts.

finished size: 7" (17.8 cm)

TECHNIQUES

Wrapped loop
Wire toggle bar

See pages 12–32 for helpful technique information.

tools

Flush cutters

Chain-nose pliers

10 mm mandrel or marker handle

Round-nose pliers

File or emery board

Chasing hammer

Steel bench block

Rotary tumbler

Polishing cloth

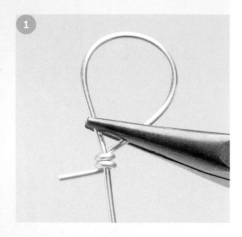

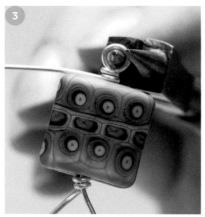

74   totally twisted

1. Flush cut 6" (15.2 cm) of 18-gauge wire. Use the mandrel to form a ½" (1.3 cm) wrapped loop about 2½" (6.4 cm) from one end of the wire. Trim any excess tail wire and file the wire end if needed.

2. Use the chasing hammer and bench block to hammer the large loop just formed. If you'd like a tooled look, use the ball-peen end of the hammer; for a flattened look, use the chasing end.

3. String the bead onto the wire and lock it in place with a ⅛" (3 mm) wide wrapped loop. Set the toggle ring aside.

4. Use the 18-gauge wire to form a toggle bar that fits inside the ½" (1.3 cm) wrapped loop formed in Step 1. Texture as desired. Set aside.

5. Cut thirty-six 1" (2.5) pieces of 18-gauge wire. Use the tip of round-nose pliers to form a loop at one of the wire's ends as you would for starting a spiral; repeat at the other wire end, making the loop curve the opposite way to create an S-shaped link about ¼" (6 mm) long. If necessary, use chain-nose pliers to pinch the S-link flat. Set aside. Make at least 36 S-links to start and more later if needed to increase the finished length of your bracelet.

6. Use chain-nose pliers to open one side of an S-link and attach it to the closed loop of another link; close the loop. Repeat to form two 5½" (14 cm) chain lengths.

7. Open the end loops of each chain and attach them to the smaller wrapped loop of the toggle ring. Attach the other end of the chains to the toggle bar.

8. Tumble the bracelet for about 30 minutes, then polish.

alternate views

Mix things up and change the shape of the toggle loop. Try a square, triangle, oval, or diamond. Any shape will work!

Instead of two lengths of the same hand-made chain, try one chain with colored wire and one with sterling silver. Or mix different styles of commercial chain.

taken
for a whirl

Create this open, airy design with a whirl of wire. If you like to wear your earrings long, simply open the empty cage wide. For shorter earrings, close the cage up tight.

TECHNIQUES

Simple loop
Open spiral
Head pin

See pages 12–32 for helpful technique information.

Flush cutters

File or emery board

Round-nose pliers

Chain-nose pliers

Rotary tumbler

Polishing cloth

materials

- 8" (20.3 cm) of sterling silver 16-gauge dead-soft wire

- 4" (10.2 cm) of sterling silver 18-gauge dead-soft wire

- 12" (30.5 cm) of sterling silver 20-gauge dead-soft wire

- 2 green 14mm lampworked glass discs

- 2 orange/red 12×16mm lampworked glass cone beads

- 2 cornflower blue 5×8mm lampworked glass rondelles

  Lampworked beads by Kerry Bogert.

finished size: 3" (7.6 cm)

1. Flush cut two 4" (10.2 cm) pieces of 16-gauge wire. File the ends smooth.

2. Use round-nose pliers to form a small loop at the end of one wire. Let the wire's natural resistance help you bend it into an open spiral.

3. Continue spiraling until you reach the the wire's center. Flip the wire and form a spiral on the other end, creating a continuous coil. Use your fingers to adjust the spiral's coils so they are equal distances apart. Make sure the starter loops on each end are somewhat centered. Set the cage aside. (Photos of this step can be seen on page 46.)

4. Repeat Steps 2 and 3 to form a second cage.

5. Tumble the finished cages for 30 minutes.

6. Use chain-nose pliers to bend the cages' starting loops to 00 degrees

7. Use the 18-gauge wire to form two 2" (5.1 cm) head pins.

8. Use 1 head pin to string 1 rondelle, 1 cone, and 1 disc. Form a simple loop to lock the beads in place; set the dangle aside. Repeat with the second head pin and remaining beads, reversing the order of the beads.

9. Use chain-nose pliers to open the bottom loop of one of the cages. Attach 1 dangle and close the loop. Repeat for the second cage and dangle.

10. Attach ear wires to the top loops of each cage.

11. Use the cloth to polish the earrings.

drip drip
drops

Long drop earrings are so much better than a leaky sink. This easy style features pairs of beads in a variety of colors. So get that hair of yours up a in a ponytail . . . you're going to want to show these off.

tools

Flush cutters

Round-nose pliers

Chain-nose pliers

File or emery board

Rotary tumbler

Polishing cloth

materials

- 14" (35.6 cm) of sterling silver 18-gauge dead-soft wire

- 8" (20.3 cm) of sterling silver 20-gauge dead-soft wire

- 2 dark blue/light blue 14×8mm lampworked rondelles

- 2 black/white striped 14×8mm lampworked rondelles

- 2 green/yellow polka-dotted 14×8mm squared lampworked rondelles

Lampworked beads by Kerry Bogert.

finished size: 2½" (6.4 cm)

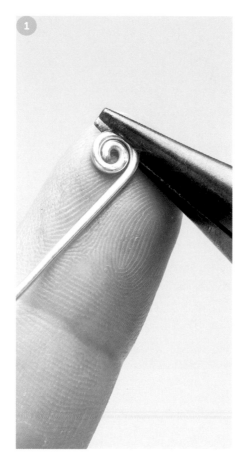

Earrings to Pendants

Pendants are really just dangle earrings on a necklace. Try using the earring tutorials on a larger scale for really cool matching pendants.

1. Flush cut 3" (7.6 cm) of 18-gauge wire. Use the tip of round-nose pliers to form a small loop at one end. Form a one-coil spiral around the initial loop to create a head pin.

2. Use the head pin to string 1 green bead. Flush cut the wire about ⅜" (9 mm) above the bead. Form a simple loop; set aside. Repeat to make a second dangle.

3. Flush cut 2" (5.1 cm) of 18-gauge wire. Form a simple loop at one end. Open the loop with chain-nose pliers and attach it to the simple loop of the green bead link.

4. Use the wire to string one of the striped beads. Flush cut the wire about ⅜" (9 mm) above the bead. Form a simple loop. Repeat connecting the second striped bead to the other green bead link.

5. Repeat Steps 3 and 4 with the blue beads. Connect one loop of a blue link to the open end of the striped link just placed. Set aside. Repeat this step to form the second earring.

6. Use the 20-gauge wire to form 2 ear wires.

7. Attach the loop of one ear wire to the open end of one of the earrings created in Step 5. Repeat for the second ear wire and earring.

8. Tumble the earrings for 20 minutes, then polish.

lasso

TECHNIQUES

Coiling
Wrapped loop
Open spiral

See pages 12–32 for helpful technique information.

I love the swoops and swirls that prance around the length of this handmade chain. With fiery orange as bright as the sun and dots as blue as the sky, this bead reminds me of the West. Just strap on your cowgirl boots, shout "Yee haw!"and you'll have roped one of these for yourself in no time.

tools

Flush cutters

1/16" (2 mm) steel mandrel

Ring mandrel

2 pairs of chain-nose pliers

File or emery board

Round-nose pliers

Rotary tumbler

Polishing cloth

materials

◟ 8' (2.4 m) of sterling silver 16-gauge dead-soft wire

◟ 3' (.9 m) of orange 20-gauge colored copper wire

◟ 1 orange/turquoise 14×33mm lampworked drop bead

Lampworked beads by Kerry Bogert.

finished size: 23" (58.4 cm)

Don't Have a Ring Mandrel?

Don't sweat it! Look around your workspace for another round object such as a tube of paint or hammer handle that has the same width.

1. Use the orange 20-gauge wire and the ¹⁄₁₆" (2 mm) mandrel to form a 3" (7.6 cm) coil. Set aside.

2. Flush cut 6" (15.2 cm) of 16-gauge wire. Slide the orange coil onto the 16-gauge wire and center it. Wrap the coiled wire around the ring mandrel to make a 1" (2.5 cm) loop.

3. Cross the bare ends of the coiled wire over each other. Use chain-nose pliers to hold the two wires at their intersection while you wrap one wire around the other twice, as if closing a wrapped loop. If necessary, use a second pair of pliers to muscle the 16-gauge into the wrap. Trim the excess wrapping wire and file the end if needed.

4. Form an open spiral with the other wire end. Gently squeeze the loop's sides if necessary to create an oval shape. Set aside.

5. Flush cut twenty-eight 3" (7.6 cm) pieces of 16-gauge wire. File the ends if needed.

6. Use the base of round-nose pliers to grasp one end of one of the wires. Form a two-wrap spiral at one end.

7. Use the base of round-nose pliers to form an open center spiral at the other wire end. Turn this spiral in the opposite direction of the first so the finished link looks like a swirly S. Set aside.

8. Repeat Steps 6 and 7 to make 28 links.

9. Attach the links together to form a 22" (55.9 cm) chain. Set aside.

10. Flush cut 5" (12.7 cm) of 16-gauge wire and file the ends if needed. Use the base of round-nose pliers to form an open spiral at one end as with the previous links.

11. Use the straight wire end to string the bead. Form a spiral at the other wire end that attaches to the open end link of the chain.

12. Tumble the necklace for 30 minutes, then polish.

framed

I love the look of finely coiled wire jewelry. What I don't love is the hours it can take to create just one component. I knew there had to be an easier way, so I developed this technique that produces several links in the same time it usually takes to make one. The best part? This technique will work for ANY shape bead!

materials

- 24' (7.3 m) of green 22-gauge colored copper wire
- 5' (1.5 m) of sterling silver 18-gauge dead-soft wire
- 4" (10.2 cm) of sterling silver 16-gauge dead-soft wire
- 5 black/green/blue 15mm lampworked lentil beads

Lampworked beads by Donna Mehnert.

finished size: 8" (20.3 cm)

TECHNIQUES

Coiling
Wrapped loop
Wrapped-loop beaded links
Hook clasp
Oxidizing

See pages 12–32 for helpful technique information.

tools

¹⁄₁₆" (2 mm) steel mandrel or size 0 knitting needle

Flush cutters

Round-nose pliers

Chain-nose pliers

File or emery board

Rotary tumbler

Polishing cloth

Liver of sulfur or hard-boiled eggs (optional)

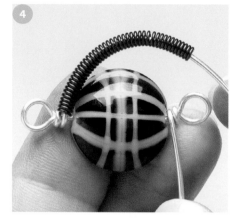

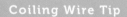

Coiling Wire Tip

When making coils, use a smaller gauge wire to wrap a larger one—it won't work the other way around. In other words, you can wrap 20-gauge wire around 18-gauge or larger, but you can't wrap it around 22- or 24-gauge. Keep that in mind when creating pendants such as these. If you want to use a heavier gauge wire, wrap it on a mandrel first and transfer the coil to your design.

1. Use 3' (0.9 m) of 22-gauge wire and the mandrel to form a coil several inches long. *Note:* The total length of coil you'll need depends on the perimeter of your beads. I suggest making a test link first and jotting down the coil measurement. This way you can make up as much coil as you think you'll need all at once. Custom cutting the pieces off a long coil will be a big time-saver!

2. Cut 8" (20.3 cm) of 18-gauge wire. Form a ¼" (6 mm) wide wrapped loop about 3" (7.6 cm) from one end of the wire; don't trim the excess wire.

3. Use the wire to string 1 bead. Form another wrapped loop that ends ⅛" (3 mm) from the top of the bead, as you need to allow some wiggle room for this design. Don't cut the excess wire. Adjust each 3" (7.6 cm) wire tail so they point in opposite directions.

4. Cut a 1" (2.5 cm) piece of coil (or other size as determined) and slide it onto one of the tail wires. Use your fingers to gently bend the coiled wire along one side of the bead. *Note:* If the coil is longer than needed, use the very tip of flush cutters to trim it to size. Be careful to avoid the 18-gauge wire inside the coil.

   Wrap the end of the 18-gauge wire around the coils of the opposite wrapped loop; trim the excess wire and file as needed.

5. Repeat Step 4 with the remaining wire tail, framing the other side of the bead.

6. Repeat Steps 2 to 5, but before wrapping the loop in Step 2, attach it to the loop of the previous link to make a chain. Repeat to connect all the beads.

7. Use the 16-gauge wire to create a hook clasp that attaches to one end of the bracelet. The loop at the bracelet's other end will act as the clasp ring.

8. If desired, oxidize the bracelet. Tumble the bracelet for 30 minutes, then polish.

alternate views

For this colorful version, use 20mm beach-glass coins framed with copper and red-colored copper wire.

split
personality

I love the look of layers, whether it's with T-shirts or necklaces. This design is fun because splitting up the beads between the two layers gives a great illusion: You can't tell where one begins and the other ends— is it just two necklaces or could there be more?

materials

- 15' (4.6 m) of sterling silver 20-gauge dead-soft wire

- 5" (12.7 cm) of sterling silver 16-gauge dead-soft wire

- 30 blue/black/clear 7×12mm lampworked glass rondelles

  Lampworked beads by Kerry Bogert.

TECHNIQUES

Wrapped loop
Wrapped-loop link
Wrapped loop, chunky style
Wire toggle clasp
Oxidizing

See pages 12–32 for helpful technique information.

tools

Flush cutters

Chain-nose pliers

Round-nose pliers

File or emery board

Rotary tumbler

Polishing cloth

Liver of sulfur

finished size: 18" (45.7 cm)

4

8

9

11

1. Flush cut 3" (7.6 cm) of 20-gauge wire. Form a wrapped loop about 1½" (3.8 cm) from one end. Trim the excess tail wire and file the end if needed.

2. Form another wrapped loop tight against the coiling of the previous loop. When closing this loop, wrap over top of the first wrapping, chunky style. Trim any excess wire and file the end if needed.

3. Repeat Steps 1 and 2, this time attaching the second loop you create to the second loop of the previous link.

4. Repeat Step 3 to make two 8" (20.3 cm) pieces of chain. Set the wire chains aside.

5. Flush cut 3" (7.6 cm) of 20-gauge wire. Form a wrapped loop at one end.

6. Slide 1 bead onto the wire. Form another wrapped loop to lock the bead in place. Set the beaded link aside.

7. Repeat Steps 4 and 5, this time attaching the second loop you create to the second loop of the previous beaded link.

8. Repeat Step 7 to make two 14-bead chains.

9. Form one beaded link that connects one end of the wire chain to one end of the beaded chain; set aside. Repeat to connect the other two chains together.

10. Use the 16-gauge wire to form a wire clasp. Set aside.

11. Arrange the chains so one has the beads on the left and the other has the beads on the right. Use the ring side of the clasp to connect the chains at one end; use the bar side of the clasp to connect the chains on the other end.

12. Oxidize the necklace, tumble for 30 minutes, then polish to highlight the wirework.

alternate views

This *Split Personality Necklace* is made with 8×14mm Czech pressed-glass beads and two different types of premade chain.

scrolliriffic

TECHNIQUES

Simple loop
Head pin
Hook clasp

See pages 12–32 for helpful technique information.

tools

Flush cutters

File or emery board

Chasing hammer

Bench block

Round-nose pliers

Chain-nose pliers

A swirling, loopy S-link can be a very elegant way to build a base for a bracelet embellished with dangles. Once you know the trick to getting the S-links shaped perfectly every time, you'll be able to make them with your eyes shut!

materials

- 18" (45.7 cm) of sterling silver 16-gauge dead-soft wire

- 8" (20.3 cm) of sterling silver 18-gauge dead-soft wire

- 6 blue 9mm anodized aluminum 20-gauge jump rings

- 6 purple 9mm anodized aluminum 20-gauge jump rings

- 4 lampworked 10×6mm glass rondelles (2 green, 1 orange, 1 light blue)

- 4 green/blue/orange 20mm lampworked glass discs

  Lampworked beads by Kerry Bogert.

finished size: 6½" (16.5 cm)

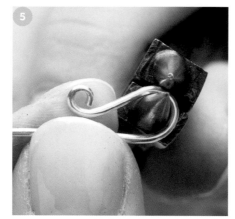

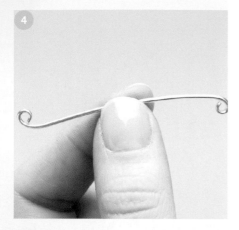

Keeping Things Consistent

To get consistent results, repeat each step of a link for the number of links you're making. For example, if you need seven links, first cut seven wire lengths, then wrap seven loops. Don't cut one, wrap one, cut one, wrap one.

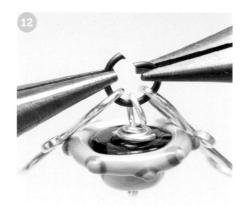

1. Flush cut five 3" (7.6 cm) pieces of 16-gauge wire. File both ends of each wire. Set aside.

2. Use a chasing hammer and bench block to flatten one of the the wires ¼" (6 mm) at each end.

3. Use the tip of round-nose pliers to form a small 2mm loop at each end of the hammered wire.

4. Use the thumb and forefinger of your nondominant hand to grasp the center of the wire so the wire's right loop points down.

5. Use the widest part of round-nose pliers to grasp the wire in the new center area between your fingers and the end loop. Form a U-shaped bend at this point.

6. Flip the link over. Position the wire as it was before with your fingers pinching the wire's center and the loop on the right pointing down. Repeat the previous step.

7. Use round-nose pliers to gently shape the S-link so it curves nicely. If desired, use the chasing hammer and bench block to slightly flatten the S-link's bends. Set aside.

8. Repeat Steps 2 to 7 to form a total of 5 S-links.

9. Flush cut four 2" (5.1 cm) pieces of 18-gauge wire. Use the wires to form 4 head pins.

10. Use 1 head pin to string 1 rondelle and disc. Form a wrapped loop to secure the beads; set aside. Repeat to make a total of 4 dangles.

11. Use the remaining 16-gauge wire to form a hook-and-eye clasp. Set aside.

12. Use 2 jump rings to attach 2 S-links together; before closing the ring, attach 1 dangle.

13. Use 2 jump rings to attach an S-link to the previously added one, adding another dangle so it sits on the same side of the S-links as the first dangle. Repeat to connect all the S-links and dangles into a chain.

14. Use 2 jump rings to attach one side of the clasp to one end of the bracelet; repeat at the other end. *Note:* Since you already work-hardened this design by hammering it, there's no need to tumble the bracelet.

To get this look, make 16 head pins and use four 12mm Tahitian-look crystal pearls, 4 Montana blue 10mm crystal rounds, and 8 light blue 8mm glass rounds to make individual dangle clusters. Finish it off by oxidizing and polishing.

refined

A design with substance, this necklace looks as great with a cocktail dress as it does with a simple tee and jeans. It's a bit of a challenge to make, but well worth the effort.

TECHNIQUES

Coiling
Wrapped loop
Hook clasp

See pages 12–32 for helpful technique information.

tools

Flush cutters

1/16" (2 mm) steel mandrel

Round-nose pliers

Chain-nose pliers

File or emery board

3/4" (1.9 cm) round mandrel or child's marker

Rotary tumbler

Polishing cloth

materials

- 40' (12.2 m) of blue 18-gauge colored copper wire

- 7' (2.1 m) of sterling silver 16-gauge dead-soft wire

- 8 blue 20 mm lampworked glass rings (10 mm inside diameter)

- 0 black/white/clear 22mm lampworked glass rings (14 mm inside diameter)

- 8 brown/gray 26mm lampworked glass rings (16 mm inside diameter)

Lampworked beads by Kerry Bogert.

finished size: 22" (55.9 cm)

1. Use 4' (1.2 m) of blue wire and the ¹⁄₁₆" (2 mm) steel mandrel to form a coil. Remove the coil and trim it to 5" (12.7 cm); set aside. Repeat to make a total of 10 coils.

2. Flush cut 8" (20.3 cm) of 16-gauge wire. Slide one of the coils onto the wire and center it.

3. Bend the coiled 16-gauge wire around the ¾" (1.9 cm) mandrel to form a U shape.

4. Slide one 22mm ring onto one side of the U-shaped wire. Pass the other side of the wire through the ring to form an X in the center of the ring.

5 Pull the two ends of uncoiled wire together until they touch and cross each other. Wrap one side of the bare wire round the other, tight against the coil, as you would a wrapped loop. The 16-gauge wire can be hard to muscle, so use chain-nose pliers if necessary to form the wrap. Trim any excess tail wire and file the end if necessary.

6 Trim the remaining 1½" (3.8 cm) of bare wire to 1" (2.1 cm). Use the base of round-nose pliers to form a large open spiral.

7 Repeat Steps 2 to 6, this time securing with a large simple loop, and using the same glass ring so the finished link has two wrapped coils locked onto the same ring. The resulting link resembles a bow tie. Set aside.

8 Repeat Steps 2 to 7, securing the coils with simple loops, to make a total of 4 ringed links with two wrapped coils each.

9 Repeat Steps 2 to 7, this time using the extra bare wire to form a hook clasp instead of the final simple loop.

10 Use chain-nose pliers to open one of the link's simple loops. Slide one 26mm ring and one 20mm ring over the loop so the rings rest on the coiled area of the link.

11 Connect the opened loop to a 22mm glass ring and close the loop again. This should trap the two glass rings from Step 9 onto the link, but still allow them to wiggle and move.

12 Repeat Steps 9 and 10, connecting a second link onto the same glass ring from Step 10.

13 Continue building the necklace, repeating Steps 9 to 11, until all the links are connected into a chain. Make sure the last link you add is the one with the hook clasp. To close, catch the clasp on the end loop of the first link.

14 Tumble the necklace for 45 minutes.

pretending

TECHNIQUES

Coiling
Wrapped loop, chunky style
Open spiral

See pages 12–32 for helpful technique information.

When I'm working on a new design I often make things up as I go, just like a kid playing pretend. You're working with a similar concept each time you create a *Pretending* necklace. This piece combines very simple links embellished with colored wire to kick up their impact. You can arrange these links in any order for a new design every time.

tools

Flush cutters

¹⁄₁₆" (2 mm) steel mandrel

Chain-nose pliers

File or emery board

Round-nose pliers

Rotary tumbler

Polishing cloth

materials

- 3' (0.9 m) of burgundy 20-gauge colored copper wire

- 3' (0.9 m) of dark green 20-gauge colored copper wire

- 3' (0.9 m) of lavender 20-gauge colored copper wire

- 3' (0.9 m) of sterling silver 20-gauge dead-soft wire

- 56" (1.4 m) of sterling silver 18-gauge dead-soft wire

- 3' (0.9 m) of sterling silver 16-gauge dead-soft wire

- 26–30 assorted 10mm to 25mm glass beads in clear, blue, green, and brown, including disc, ring, and wide-hole shapes

  Lampworked beads by Jill Symons.

finished size: 47" (1.2 m)

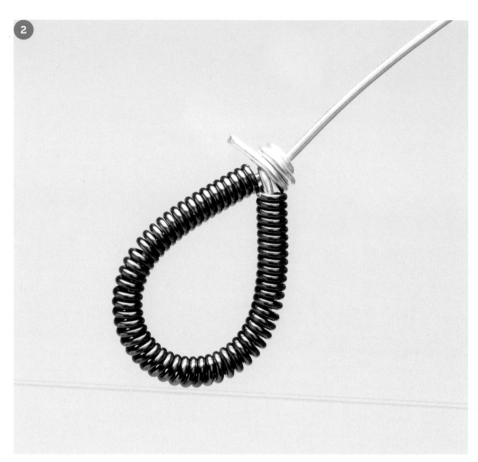

1. *Make Link 1:* Use 2' (61 cm) of lavender 20-gauge wire and the mandrel to form a coil. Slip the coil off the mandrel and trim it to 2" (5.1 cm).

2. Use the base of round-nose pliers to form a U-shaped bend in the wire. Slide the coil onto the wire and center it over the bend. Squeeze the wire so the coil ends touch. Wrap the short exposed 18-gauge wire around the longer one at the edge of the coils, creating a chunky-style wrapped loop.

3. Use the open end of the wire to string one 25mm bead; lock it in place with a regular chunky-style wrapped loop. Set Link 1 aside.

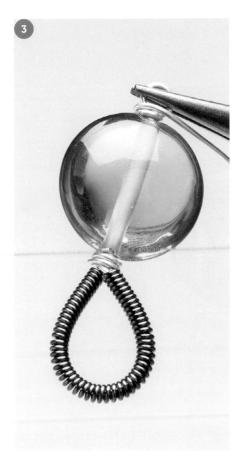

Watch Out for Flying Wire!

This project has a lot of cutting and snipping going on, so you'll want to keep those cut ends from flying all over your bead room. When you're about to flush cut a piece of wire, lay your index finger over top the wire you're about to cut. Don't worry, you won't snip yourself. Flush cutters have a V-shaped blade and you're putting your finger over the wide top, not the cutting area on the bottom. Don't forget to wear your safety glasses!

4. *Make Link 2:* Use 12" of sterling silver 20-gauge wire and the mandrel to form a coil. Slide the coil off the mandrel and trim it to 1" (2.5 cm). Set aside.

5. Flush cut 6" (15.2 cm) of 18-gauge wire. Form a wrapped loop about 2" (5.1 cm) from one end of the wire.

6. Use the straight end of the wire to string 1 spacer bead, 1 disc bead, the sterling coil, and 1 spacer bead. Form a wrapped loop that attaches to the coil end of Link 1. Trim any excess wire and file if needed.

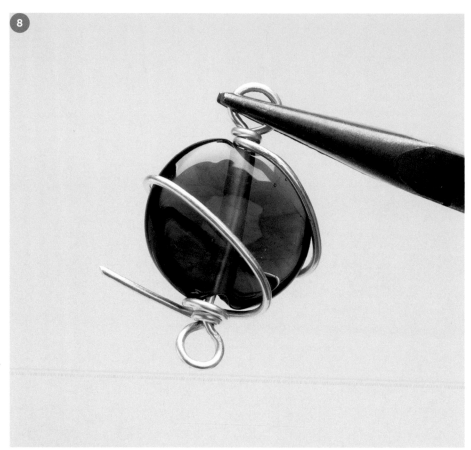

7 *Make Link 3:* Flush cut 8" (20.3 cm) of 18-gauge wire. Form a wrapped loop about 2" (5.1 cm) from one wire end. Trim the excess tail wire.

8 Slide on one 20mm bead and form another wrapped loop; don't trim the wire. Use the extra wire to coil around the side of the bead twice. Finish the wire by wrapping around the base of the first wrapped loop. Trim any excess wire and file the end if necessary. *Note:* Make this link separately, then connect it to the chain with other links or attach the second loop to the chain's end link before wrapping it closed.

9 *Make Link 4:* Use 12" (30.5 cm) of dark green 20-gauge wire and the mandrel to form a coil. Slide the coil off the mandrel and trim it to ½" (1.3 cm). Set aside.

10 Flush cut 6" (15.2 cm) of 16-gauge wire. Form a two-coil open spiral at one end of the wire.

11 Use chain-nose pliers to grasp the straight length of wire and form a 90-degree bend at the base of the spiral so the spiral looks like a lollipop.

12 String one 15mm bead, the dark green coil, and one 10mm bead on the wire.

13 Use chain-nose pliers to form another sharp bend in the wire, locking your beads in place. Form another open center spiral with the remaining length of wire. *Note:* This type of link is made separately, then connected to the chain with other links.

14 Continue forming and connecting links end to end, creating various combinations of Links 1 to 4. Mix and match different parts of the other links to create one-of-a-kind links. For example, use the large coiled loop from Link 1 at one end and an open spiral from Link 4 at the opposite end. Or make a Link 3-style caged bead on one end and a bar bell–style at the other end as in Link 2.

Continue building until you have a 30" (76.2 cm) chain.

15 Finish the necklace by simply attaching the last link to the first link.

16 Tumble the necklace for 45 minutes.

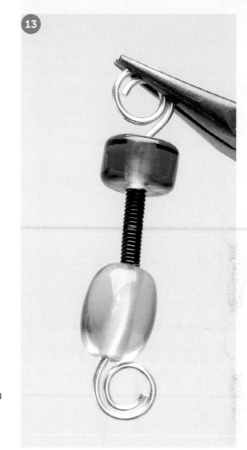

13

flying
trapeze

Don't you just love the swoon and whoosh you feel when watching a daring acrobat swing through the air? This pendant is an ode to the circus and a reminder to have a little fun with your functional jewelry. The bead can spin and flip while it's worn so you can imagine your own trapeze acts.

materials

- 4" (10.2 cm) of sterling silver 16-gauge dead-soft wire

- 4" (10.2 cm) of sterling silver 18-gauge dead-soft wire

- 12" (30.5 cm) of red 20-gauge colored copper wire

- 1 red 9mm anodized aluminum jump ring

- 1 red/white/clear 25×21mm hollow lampworked round with a striped 10×5mm bead inside

- 2 sterling silver 5mm smart beads

Lampworked beads by Kerry Bogert.

finished size: *pendant*, 2" (5.1 cm)

TECHNIQUES

Simple loop
Coiling

See pages 12–32 for helpful technique information.

tools

Flush cutters

Round-nose pliers

1/16" (2 mm) steel mandrel

Chain-nose pliers

Chasing hammer

Bench block

Polishing cloth

1

Something to Remember

You can always harden wire, but it takes a torch to soften hard wire. With that in mind, it's best to buy dead-soft!

4

5a

5b

1. Flush cut 3" (7.6 cm) of 18-gauge wire. Form a 3mm simple loop at one end. Use the wire to string the hollow bead, catching the inner bead before you exit the second hole. Flush cut the wire to ⅜" (9 mm) above the bead. Form another simple loop to secure the beads. Set the beaded link aside.

2. Use 12" (30.5 cm) of 20-gauge wire and the mandrel to form a coil. Slide the coil off the mandrel and trim to 1" (2.5 cm). Set aside.

3. Cut 4" (10.2 cm) of 16-gauge wire. Use round-nose pliers to form a U shape with the wire. Use the chasing hammer and bench block to flatten the point of the bend until flat.

4. String 1 smart bead, the coil, and 1 smart bead onto one side of the U-shaped wire. Insert the wire ends into the simple loops of the beaded link.

5. Form a 4mm loop at each end of the U-shaped wire. Make the loops just wide enough that the beaded link's simple loops can't slip off.

6. Attach the jump ring to the bend of the U-shape to create a bail.

7. Finish with a little polishing; hang from your favorite chain.

hook, line,
and sinker

TECHNIQUES

Wrapped loop
Coiling
Opening/closing jump rings

*See pages 12–32 for helpful
technique information.*

Fringe is fun, fringe is fabulous, and you can create fringe for metal jewelry with jump rings. These little wire doodads echo the shape of this gorgeous lampworked bead, and the pop of an orange-colored coil adds just the right visual touch.

tools

Flush cutters

Round-nose pliers

2 pairs of
chain-nose pliers

File or emery board

Rotary tumbler

Polishing cloth

materials

- 10' (3.1 m) of sterling silver 20-gauge dead-soft wire

- 2' (61 cm) of orange 20-gauge colored copper wire

- 30 blue 9mm anodized aluminum 18-gauge jump rings

- 1 blue/green/purple/orange 43mm lampworked donut with 18mm hole

Lampworked beads by Carter Seibels.

finished size: 17" (43.2 cm)

117

1. Cut thirty-six 3" (7.6 cm) pieces of silver wire. Form a wrapped loop at one end of 1 wire. Trim the excess tail wire.

2. Form a second wrapped loop tight against the coils of the previous loop. When you're ready to wrap this loop, overlap the previous wrapping. Trim the excess wire and file any sharp ends.

3. Repeat Steps 1 and 2, attaching the first loop of each new link to the second loop of the previous link, until you've created 3' (0.9 m) of chain.

4. Slide the chain through the bead's hole and bring the ends together.

5 Flush cut 8" (20.3 cm) of silver wire. Form a wrapped loop about 2" (5.1 cm) from one wire end that attaches to both end loops of the chain.

6 Measure 2¼" (5.7 cm) down the wire from the wrapped loop just made. Use your fingers to form a hairpin bend in the wire. Use chain-nose pliers to pinch the arch of the bend tight.

7 Use chain-nose pliers to grasp the 2 pieces of wire running along side each other near the coil of the wrapped loop. Wrap the free wire end around the first wrapping as you did with the chain links. Trim the excess wire and file any sharp ends.

9

10

11

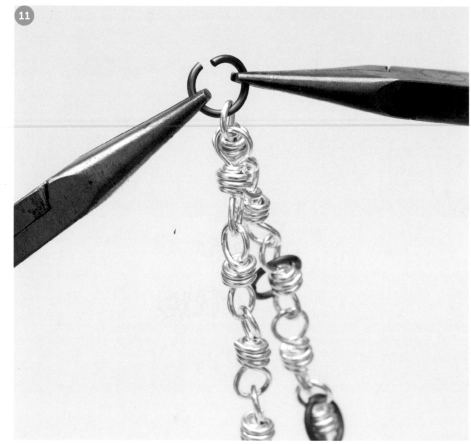

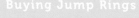

Buying Jump Rings

When ordering commercial jump rings, their size is based on the inside diameter of the ring. Watch what gauge wire you're choosing and note the diameter, too. This is more important for projects involving chain mail, but an important detail all the same.

8 Use a 24" (61 cm) piece of orange wire and the mandrel to form a coil. Slide the coil off the mandrel and trim it to 2" (5.1 cm).

9 Slide the 2" (5.1 cm) coil onto the hook. Use chain-nose pliers to bend the ¼" (6 mm) of exposed silver wire back onto the orange coil; this will lock the coil onto the hook.

10 Use your fingers to form a U-shaped bend in the hook. The hook is used to connect to the focal bead when worn.

11 Connect 1 jump ring to the second loop of every other chain link. For fuller fringe, just keep adding more rings. You can make it as fringy as you like.

12 Tumble the necklace for 45 minutes, then polish.

alternate views

To make this slightly longer version of the necklace, skip Steps 1 through 3 and use 18" (45.7 cm) of premade 2.7mm flat cable chain. Instead of a lampworked donut, use a jet 30mm crystal ring and get a thicker fringed look by adding black and silver jump rings to every link in the chain for the 2" (5.1 cm) closest to the hook and ring.

timeless

I know this design isn't timeless in the classical sense.
I can't image a 1920s movie starlet wearing one, but I
could be wrong. The bracelet gets its name from the
large flat disc bead that looks very much like a watch
face on your wrist. Obviously glass can't tell time
though, so it's *Timeless*!

materials

- 13" (33 cm) of sterling silver 16-gauge dead-soft wire

- 2' (61 cm) of sterling silver 18-gauge dead-soft wire

- 4' (1.2 m) of amethyst, lavender, or silver 18-gauge colored copper wire

- 2' (61 cm) of orange, Pacific blue, or amethyst 20-gauge colored copper wire

- 2 sterling silver 5mm smart beads

- 1 dark blue/light blue/orange 34mm lampworked disc bead

  Lampworked beads by Kerry Bogert.

finished size: 7" (17.8 cm)

TECHNIQUES

Simple loop
Coiling
Spiral

See pages 12–32 for helpful technique information.

tools

Flush cutters

File or emery board

Round-nose pliers

Chain-nose pliers

1/16" (2 mm) steel mandrel

Bracelet mandrel or pint glass

Nylon mallet

Bench block

Rotary tumbler

Polishing cloth

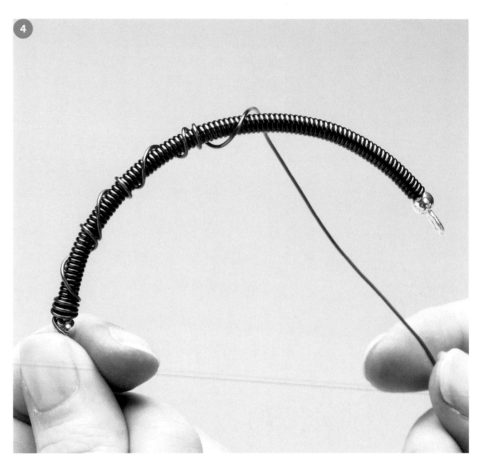

4

Try This!

If you use a longer piece of 16-gauge wire for the core wire, you can style this design up a bit: Instead of forming simple loops at each end to secure the components, form large hole, open spirals. One of these will make a great-looking catch for your clasp.

1 Flush cut and file the ends of 7" (17.8 cm) of sterling silver 16-gauge wire. Form a simple loop at one end. Set aside.

2 Use the mandrel and 4' (1.2 m) of 18-gauge colored copper wire to form a 5" (12.7 cm) coil. Flush cut the ends and file if needed. Set aside. *Note:* You can adjust the finished size of this bangle by shortening or lengthening this measurement.

3 String 1 smart bead onto the 16-gauge wire and slide it to the simple loop. String the coil and 1 smart bead. Trim the excess 16-gauge wire to ¾" (1.9 cm) past the final smart bead. Form another simple loop to lock the components in place.

4 Cut 12" (30.5 cm) of 20-gauge wire. Wrap this wire over the entire length of the 18-gauge coil to embellish it.

5 Bend the coiled wire around the bracelet mandrel to shape it. Set the band aside.

6 Form the clasp in a *snail link* style. This type of link is made in 2 pieces: the shell, made up of a spiral; and the head, which passes through the spiral. For this project, the head acts as the hook part of the clasp. Start by flush cutting 6" (15.2 cm) of 16-gauge wire. Form a spiral at each end of the wire. Leave 2" (5.1 cm) gap between the spirals.

6

Snail Link Size

You can make this link as large or small as you like. Simply adjust the length of the 16-gauge wire to fit the size of your spirals. Large spirals will need a longer piece of wire and smaller spirals require a shorter piece.

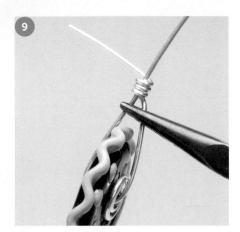

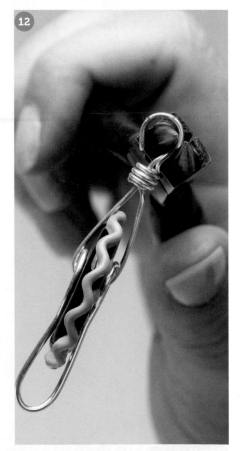

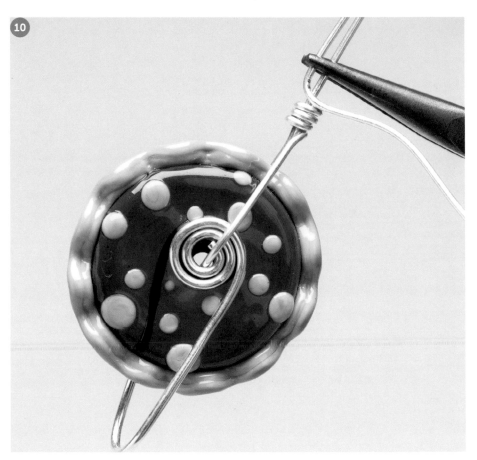

totally twisted

7 Use the base of round-nose pliers to grasp the 16-gauge wire the center; bend it into a U shape. Use your fingers to line up the centers of the spirals. Use the nylon mallet and bench block to work-harden the bend so it holds its shape.

8 Flush cut 10" (25.4 cm) of sterling silver 18-gauge wire; set aside. Wrap the 16-gauge wire around the disc bead so its spirals align with the bead hole. Slide the 18-gauge wire through the holes of the spirals and disc bead. Extend the 18-gauge wire about two-thirds of the way through the spirals and bead.

9 Use your fingers to bend the 18-gauge wire ends toward each other. Use chain-nose pliers to grasp the two wires where they cross. Use your opposite hand to tightly wrap the shorter wire around the longer one. Make the wraps about ¼" (6 mm) from the disc bead's edge. Trim the excess tail wire and file if needed.

10 Measure 1" (2.5 cm) down the 18-gauge wire from the wraps and fold the wire back on itself at that point. Use chain-nose pliers to pinch the bend tight.

11 Use chain-nose pliers to grasp the two parallel wires close to the wraps. Wrap the free end of the wire over the top of the first wraps. Trim any excess tail wire and file if needed.

12 Use round-nose pliers to bend the double wires into a hook that points to the underside of the focal bead. *Note:* The hook may snag on things if facing up.

13 Open one of the simple loops on the band. Close it around the hammered bend of the snail link. The hook side of the snail link should easily reach the other loop in the band to close the bangle.

14 Tumble the bracelet for 30 minutes, then polish.

13

the eyes
have it

Go to great lengths to create drama and pizzazz. Extra-long necklaces, ranging from thirty to forty inches (76.2 cm to 1 m), do just that. Not only is this design eye-catching, it's versatile, too: You can double it up for another look or triple wrap it on your wrist for a funky bracelet.

materials

- 8' (2.4 m) of sterling silver 16-gauge dead-soft wire
- 8 black/purple/pink 21mm lampworked-glass lentil beads

Lampworked beads by Kerry Bogert.

finished size: 34" (86.4 cm)

TECHNIQUES

Simple loop
Simple-loop bead link

See pages 12–32 for helpful technique information.

tools

Flush cutters

File or emery board

Round-nose pliers

Chain-nose pliers

Ruler

Rotary tumbler

Cleaning solution

Liver of sulfur or hard-boiled eggs

Polishing cloth

Saving Chain

You'll start this piece by making the chain that links the beads together. If you end up with more than you need, save it! Chain is great to have on hand for all sorts of jewelry-making projects.

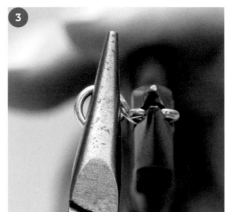

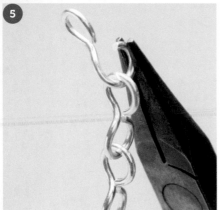

1. Flush cut forty-eight 1½" (3.8 cm) pieces of wire. File all the ends smooth.

2. Use the large base of your round-nose pliers to grasp one end of one of the wires. Roll the wire in toward the center, as you would to make a simple loop. Do the same on the other wire end, rolling the loop in the opposite direction to form a figure-eight link.

3. Use two pairs of chain-nose pliers to grasp each loop of the link. Hold one loop steady while you make a half twist with the other, making the loops perpendicular. Set the link aside.

4. Repeat Steps 2 and 3 to make a total of 48 links.

5. Use chain-nose pliers to open one of the loops on a link. Attach the link to a second link and close the loop. Continue until you've connected 6 links into a short chain; set aside. Repeat to form a total of 8 chains.

6. Tumble the chains for about 30 minutes. Set the chains aside.

7. Flush cut 3" (7.6 cm) of wire. File one end. Form a simple loop at that end.

8. Slide 1 bead onto the wire. Trim the exposed wire to ¾" (1.9 cm) above the bead and file the end smooth. Form a simple loop to lock the bead in place. Set the beaded link aside.

9 Repeat Steps 7 and 8 seven times to make a total of 8 beaded links.

10 Use chain-nose pliers to connect the chain pieces to the beaded links, forming a long chain. Connect the last beaded link to the end of the first chain to form a circle.

11 Oxidize the necklace and polish.

alternate views

For this extra-long version, make additional chain and use 10 fuchsia 16×20mm Czech glass pebbles. Form the beaded links with extra wire for the second wrapped loop and coil it around the sides of the bead, creating a wire cage. To finish off the cage, simply coil over the first wrapped loop and trim any excess wire.

twirl-a-gig
necklace

TECHNIQUES

Simple loop
Spiral
Coiling
Wrapped loop
Wire clasp

See pages 12–32 for helpful technique information.

Disc beads are my absolute favorite to make. The possibilities for the layers are limitless. Though the flat side is usually the most fabulous side, the decorated edge of a disc can really ROCK! This design lets those edges get the attention they deserve.

materials

- 43" (1.1 m) of sterling silver 16-gauge dead-soft wire

- 6' (1.8 m) of sterling silver 18-gauge dead-soft wire

- 3' (0.9 m) of Pacific blue 20-gauge colored copper wire

- 3' (0.9 m) of orange 20-gauge colored copper wire

- 3' (0.9 m) of red 20-gauge colored copper wire

- 3' (0.9 m) of yellow 20-gauge colored copper wire

- 3' (0.9 m) of green 20-gauge colored copper wire

- 10 bright-colored 18mm to 26mm lampworked-glass disc beads to match wire

- 10 bright-colored 10×6mm lampworked-glass rondelles to match discs

Lampworked beads by Kerry Bogert.

finished size: 19¾" (50.2 cm)

Note: This design is styled to match Cagey on page 44.

tools

Flush cutters

File or emery board

Round-nose pliers

Chain-nose pliers

¹⁄₁₆" (2 mm) steel mandrel

Rotary tumbler

Polishing cloth

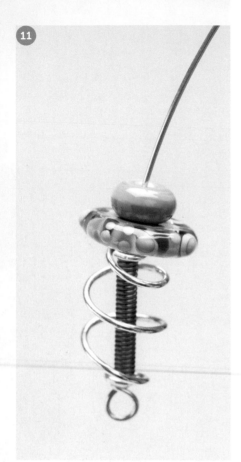

1. Flush cut ten 4" (10.2 cm) pieces of 16-gauge wire. File the ends smooth.

2. Use round-nose pliers to form a simple loop at the end of one of the 16-gauge wire pieces. Let the wire's natural resistance help you bend it, forming an open spiral.

3. Continue spiraling until you reach the wire's center. Turn the wire over and form a simple loop at the other end. Spiral this side in toward the center. When the link is close to complete, put your pliers down and do a little hand forming. If necessary, adjust the bends so they are equal distances apart. Also make sure the simple loops are somewhat centered. Set the cage aside. (Photos of these steps can be see on page 46.)

4 Repeat Steps 2 and 3 to make a total of 10 cages.

5 Tumble the cages for 30 minutes. Set aside.

6 Use one of the 20-gauge colored wires and the mandrel to form a coil. Slide the coil off the mandrel and flush cut the ends.

7 Cut the coil into 1" (2.5 cm) lengths. Set the coils aside.

8 Repeat Steps 6 and 7 for each of the colored wires. You should end up with about a dozen coils. *Note:* You won't end up using all the coils in this project, but save them to make *Cagey*, page 44.

9 Flush cut 6" (15.2 cm) of 18-gauge wire. Form a wrapped loop 2" (5.1 cm) from one end. Trim any excess tail wire and file if needed.

10 Slide 1 coil inside 1 cage. Line up the cage's starting loops with the coil's hole. You may need to pull the cage lengthwise to get it around the coil. We'll call this piece "Coil 'n Cage."

11 Use the 18-gauge wire to string the Coil 'n Cage, 1 disc bead, and 1 rondelle. Close the link with another wrapped loop.

12 Repeat Steps 9 and 10, this time connecting the first wrapped loop to the second loop of the previous link.

13 Repeat Step 12 to connect all the components. Set the chain aside.

14 Use the remaining 16-gauge wire to make a simple S clasp. Attach the clasp to the end of the chain. The first wrapped loop will act as the catch for the clasp.

15 Tumble the necklace for 30 minutes, then polish.

alternate views

This monochromatic version of *Twirl-A-Gig* uses purple vintage 16mm crackle-glass beads and purple-colored copper wire.

unhinged

I often design pieces specifically to be played with; it puts the FUN in functional! This bracelet design begs to be fiddled while you drive, wait in line at the grocery store, or have long chats with girlfriends on the phone . . . you just can't keep still while you wear it.

materials

- 12" (30.5 cm) of sterling silver 14-gauge dead-soft wire

- 3' (.9 m) of sterling silver 18-gauge dead-soft wire

- 3' (.9 m) of blue 18-gauge colored copper wire

- 2' (61 cm) of sterling silver 20-gauge dead-soft wire

- 4 sterling silver 5mm smart beads

- 4 bright-colored 14mm lampworked disc beads

- 2 bright-colored 14mm lampworked beads with ¼" (6 mm) holes

  Lampworked beads by Kerry Bogert.

finished size: 9" (22.9 cm) (to accommodate large beads)

TECHNIQUES

Simple loop
Coiling

See pages 12–32 for helpful technique information.

tools

Flush cutters

File or emery board

Round-nose pliers

Chain-nose pliers

¹⁄₁₆" (2 mm) steel mandrel

Chasing hammer

Steel bench block

Rotary tumbler

Polishing cloth

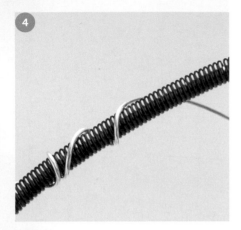

4

Why the Second Coil Layer?

You don't have to add the second layer of wire over the 18-gauge coils, but it helps avoid wear on the colored copper. If you don't add it, the large-holed bead will rub away the color coating as it slides along the coil.

1. Flush cut two 6" (15.2 cm) pieces of 14-gauge wire. File the ends smooth. Form a ¼" (6 mm) simple loop on one end of each piece. Set aside.

2. Use the sterling silver 18-gauge wire and the mandrel to create a 2½" to 3" (6.4 to 7.6 cm) coil. Remove from the mandrel and trim the ends. Repeat this step using the blue 18-gauge wire.

3. Use one of the 14-gauge wires to string 1 smart bead, 1 disc bead, and one of the coils; slide the beads and coil down to the simple loop. Repeat for the second 14-gauge wire. Set aside.

4. Cut 12" (30.5 cm) of 20-gauge wire. Use the wire to wrap a second coiled layer over the entire length of one of the 18-gauge coils. Repeat for the second 18-gauge coil. Set these "hinge halves" aside.

5. Use one of the hinge halves to string 1 large-holed bead, 1 disc bead, and 1 smart bead; snug the disc and smart beads down to the coils. Set aside. Repeat with the other hinge half.

6. Trim the exposed 14-gauge wire of one of the hinge halves to ¾" (1.9 cm); file the end smooth. Form a ¼" (6 mm) simple loop. Set aside.

7. Use the tip of chain-nose pliers to grasp the exposed 14-gauge wire of the other hinge half close to the last bead. Form a 45-degree bend.

8. Grasp the wire about ½" (1.3 cm) up from the bend with the base of round-nose pliers. Wrap the wire around the pliers to form a hook. Trim the wire even with the 45-degree bend. Flush cut any excess wire; file the end smooth. Use the tip of chain-nose pliers to form a slight bend at the wire's tip.

9. Use the chasing hammer and bench block to flatten the arch of the hook. Be careful to keep the beads off the edge of the block so they aren't damaged by the hammer.

10. Open one of the simple loops and connect it to the simple loop of the second hinge half.

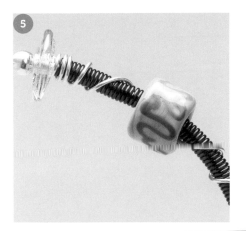

11 Use your fingers to form a gentle bend in each hinge half to follow the shape of your wrist. *Note:* You may need to twist one of the simple loops so the clasp will function properly. Simply grasp the loop with chain-nose pliers and twist it to the proper position.

12 Tumble the bracelet for 30 minutes, then polish.

Mix and Match

You can make several different hinge halves for this bracelet design and interchange them. Just open up the simple loop at the hinge and switch out the half. You can have extra fun by adding more then one large hole slider bead, too.

beadmakers

When it comes to glass beads, no two are ever exactly alike; the same goes for the artists who make them. There are beadmakers in every corner of the world—here are those you'll find in this book.

cassie donlen

Cassie has been a lampwork artist and jewelry designer for the past seven years. She describes her work as having a very bright, whimsical feel. Cassie lives in St. Louis, Missouri, with her husband and three sons. Her lampworked beads and jewelry can be purchased at glassbeadle.com. Cassie recently started a website that is dedicated specifically for beaders and jewelry designers. All sorts of supplies, lessons, and kits are available at ticklemebeads.com. Cassie's beads are used in *BANG Gals,* page 36.

libby leuchtman

Libby has been making glass beads for twelve years. After making beads on her own for two years, she took her first class with Tom and Sage Holland. Years later she started her own teaching studio in her bead store and eventually became the Director of Torchworking for Third Degree Glass Factory in St. Louis, Missouri (stlglass.com). Libby finds glass to have endless possibilities, and it continues to fascinate her every time she lights the torch. Libby's beads are used in *Catching A Wave,* page 48.

donna mehnert

Donna has been playing with beads since she was a little kid, stringing seed beads and cutting up old strands of beads she found in her mom's jewelry drawer. She's been making her own glass beads since 2001 and has traveled to Italy and Germany to study and teach. She gravitates toward unusual color combinations and often adds a touch of gold for some groovy sparkle. Donna has lived in Texas for over thirty years and digs working in her butterfly garden. You can learn more about her and read her ramblings at blackberrybeads.com. Donna's beads are used in *Framed,* page 88.

melanie moertel

Born in 1976 in Erlangen, Germany, Melanie lives as a full-time lampworker in downtown Bamberg. Her previous career was working as a graphic designer before turning to glass beads in 2003. She works on a Bobcat (torch) in the studio in her apartment and makes a living from selling beads and teaching lampworking. All of Melanie's beads are made with soft glass, and she likes to work in a very detailed and colorful style. To contact her or read more about her beads, go to melaniemoertel.de. Melanie's beads are used in *Chunky Monkey,* page 52.

sarah moran

Sarah has always liked beads. It started when her aunt showed her how to weave seed beads on a loom when Sarah was eight years old. She rediscovered beads when she was sixteen. It just so happened that Sarah's mom liked beads, too, so she had an instant companion to hunt the bead aisles with. After she acquired every bead she wanted from the shops, she still needed more. That's when her Mom told her about *Making Glass Beads* by Cindy Jenkins, and the rest is history. Sarah's beads can be found at z-beads.com and are used in *Butterfly,* page 40, and *Squiggle Wiggle,* page 68.

anne ricketts

Anne has dabbled in every kind of art and craft, from painting and woodworking to ceramics and silver work. She was an avid quilter for thirteen years before she started making glass beads and finds she still gets a lot of inspiration from the fabrics in her stash. Anne lives in central Texas with her husband and three sons. They also have a daughter who has blessed them with a beautiful grandson! To find out more about Anne's beads, visit her website at amrglassworks.net. Anne's beads are used in *Fantasticness,* page 72.

carter seibels

Carter is a glass-bead artist and jewelry designer living in Berkeley, California. Her love of color and all things bright and shiny has led her down a path full of creative endeavors. On most days you can find Carter on a walk with her golden retriever Finn or at the torch making bright colorful beads. For more information or to reach Carter, visit divaliglassjewelry.com or e-mail her at sales@divaliglassjewelry.com. Carter's beads are used in *Hook, Line, and Sinker,* page 116.

jill symons

Jill's beads are graphically simple and quite modern, as she "allows" the glass itself to always be front and center. Her beads display the glass's beauty through the release of color and sparkle. Jill has been creating lampworked beads for over a decade and each session at the torch is magical, as it should always be. She works mostly with Lauscha glass, imported by her father at glassdaddy.com. Find Jill's work at jillsymons.com. Jill's beads are used in *Pretending,* page 106.

To find out more about learning to make glass beads, visit The International Society of Glass Beadmakers (isgb.org). This is a nonprofit organization dedicated to promoting, supporting, and educating the art of making handcrafted glass beads.

resources

The Beadin' Path
(207) 865-4785
beadinpath.com
For glass beads and findings.

Bead Trust LLC
(510) 540-5815
beadtrust.com
For glass beads and findings.

Beaducation
(650) 654-7791
beaducation.com
For online tutorials, wire supplies,
and tools.

Blue Buddha Boutique
(866) 602-7464
bluebuddhaboutique.com
For colorful jump rings.

Fire Mountain Gems
(800) 423-2319
firemountaingems.com
For tools.

Jewelry Supply
(916) 780-9610
jewelrysupply.com
For smart beads.

Out On A Whim
(707) 664-8343
whimbeads.com
For seed beads.

Paramount Wire Company
(973) 672-0500
parawire.com
For colored wire and coiling tools.

Rio Grande
(800) 545-6566
riogrande.com
For findings, sterling silver wire,
and tools.

Self-Representing Artists
self-representing-artist.com
Find out more about self-representing
glass artists and literally hundreds
of websites for makers of handmade
glass beads.

Thunderbird Supply
(800) 545-7968
thunderbirdsupply.com
For sterling silver wire and tools.

Tickle Me Beads
ticklemebeads.com
For online tutorials, glass beads,
and tools.

index

Create beautiful designs
with these inspiring resources
from Interweave

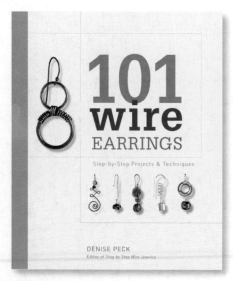
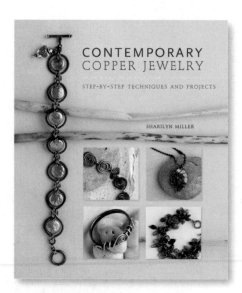
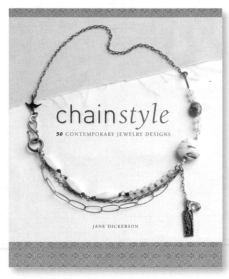